Undoubtedly
Awesome

Undoubtedly Awesome

YOUR OWN PERSONAL ROADMAP FROM DOUBT TO FLOW

Anne Tucker

ISBN: 0692823883
ISBN 13: 9780692823880
Library of Congress Control Number: XXXXX (If applicable)
LCCN Imprint Name: City and State (If applicable)

Table of Contents

Introduction

You may have heard the phrase "thoughts become things". It gets to the idea that each of us creates our lives through our thoughts. Your thoughts create your abundance of good things in your life; your relationships, the success of your business or career, even the kind of home and family you have.

You are always creating, whether you are trying to or not, simply by the power of your thoughts. You can create passively, just by staying in the thinking ruts that you've developed from your beliefs and habits. Or you can create actively and deliberately, through the mechanism that focuses and directs your creative power. That mechanism is your decisions.

Decision making a powerful tool for deliberately creating the life you want. When you make a decision, it focuses and directs your attention on whatever you are trying to create, and where your attention goes, everything else follows. Everything you do starts with a decision, and whatever decision you make determines what comes next.

However, despite the fact that you may be a great decision maker, your decision process might not always work perfectly. Sometimes doubt may creep into your decisions and prevent you from following through with your decisions, or from enjoying your decisions. Doubt can be one of your biggest barriers to creating the life you want.

This book will help to free you from that doubt by developing your awareness of your own decision process. What makes this book even more powerful is that the answers you'll find will be tailored specifically to you – how you think, solve problems, and make decisions, based on your own soul type. You'll be able to identify and read about your soul type. When you do, you'll recognize yourself clearly, and you'll see your own thought process in a whole new way. You'll see how the way that you think – the specific and personal decision process that you use every day – may be creating doubt and ambiguity for you.

What's great about becoming self-aware is that awareness IS the cure. You don't have to add another ten minutes of affirmations in the morning, or go deeper, or meditate longer. Once you see yourself clearly, you can't un-see it again, so the work is done. With your new awareness, you will notice when you are making choices in a way that is going to create doubt in your mind, and you'll know what to do differently.

So buckle up, get excited, and read on because, if you do, an hour from now you will know yourself better, understand yourself better, and doubt yourself less often than you do right now. And your life will be better because of it.

Part One
Decisions

CHAPTER 1

Doubt and Flow

I spent today in doubt, and it was miserable. I was trying to rewrite this chapter and I wasn't sure how to tell you, in a clear, succinct way, what this book is about. It was easier to write the whole book than it was to sum it up in one, short paragraph. (Okay, that's not true. But it felt that way today.) I was doubting myself because I just couldn't put my finger on the best way to tell you how impactful the learning in this book has been for me, and how impactful it will be for you. I was yo-yoing back and forth all day between descriptions that I didn't really like, and I worked my way into a complete funk. I began to doubt that I would ever be able to get it finished. I wallowed in regret and ate most of my secret chocolate stash, lamenting the wasted years I spent trying to write it. And as I left my office and dejectedly put my things in the trunk of my car, it hit me. Right in that moment, as if it was meant to show me the way, I was living the point of this book. And here it is, nice and clear and succinct:

This book is about freeing yourself from doubt. This book will give you a road map, specifically tailored to you and how you think, that will show you where you develop doubt, how it weasels into your thoughts, and how you can conquer it so that you can hold space for what you want long enough for the world to catch up.

Just like me, you urgently need this book, because a part of your life isn't working. The part of your life I'm talking about is where ever dissatisfaction and doubt are making you spin in circles, feeling dissatisfied with whatever you have, or stuck in doubt about what you should do. Where in your life do you feel that way? Is it your career, your relationship, where you live, or some other decision you're struggling with?

You've probably tried to fix this part of your life, to grow and reach for something bigger or more meaningful, or that fits you better. The problem is that when you're stepping out of your comfort zone, reaching for the identity, the work, the relationship or the life that you truly want for yourself and feel in your heart is where you should be, you are particularly vulnerable to doubt. The more important it is to you, the more exposed and fragile you feel. In those moments doubt can be a very destructive feeling. Doubt can be a big bucket of cold water that gets poured over whatever fire you're trying to ignite. It makes you feel small, weak, vulnerable and afraid. It can kill your dreams, steal your hope, and destroy your relationships.

I'm not saying that all doubt is bad. A little doubt can be a good thing if it keeps you humble and careful. Sometimes a little doubt will whisper in the back of your mind just in time to keep you from buying those too-skinny jeans, and later you will thank your doubt. But too much doubt can paralyze you. When doubt starts to become part of more and more of your decisions, or takes hold in your important life choices, you can end up feeling dissatisfied and unhappy with whatever you choose. And when you feel bad about your life choices, you feel bad about yourself.

Flow - What It Could Be

When you learn where your doubt is coming from and how to get rid of it, it's like taking the chains off of your dreams. It makes space for things to grow. And because you're not always questioning the choices you make, it gives you a new perspective of gratitude for the life you have now.

The more doubt you purge from your life, the more you can begin to feel in flow. I think of flow as the effortless, synchronistic unfolding of your life in a way that moves you toward the life you were meant to live. When you're in flow, it feels like success is inevitable, like the thing you are trying to build or make is already accomplished, a foregone conclusion, and you are just connecting the dots between you and your awesome future. It feels like you are aligned with the universe, everything you need is flowing toward you and all you have to do is stand in the river and catch it as it floats by. Who wouldn't want more of that?

I've been in flow for the last few months. I'm finally working on the things that I feel called to do, and the universe seems to be lining up to pave my way forward. I see it in small ways every day. For example, I keep a list of the people I need to call in a day in order to keep different projects rolling, and now those people are surprising me by calling me first, or even stopping by my house because they were in the neighborhood. People with the skills I need are showing up in my life and offering to help me. I've felt peaceful, joyful and more effective. All these good things were making me feel in flow until today, when doubt hit me like a ton of bricks and the flow just stopped. And I felt first-hand the effects of doubt.

Stuck and Spinning In Circles

You want to free yourself from doubt so you can get back into flow. To do that, you have to begin by looking where doubt starts – in your decisions.

Often, doubt starts because your decisions get overwhelmed with ambiguity. When you make a decision, you rely on your decision process to reduce any ambiguity you have about which choice to make. Your decision process is specific to you and, when it works well, it gives you just the right balance of input from the outside world such as data or recommendations, and your own, internal guidance which helps you see which option or path feels best to you.

When you're trying really hard to make the best decision, sometime that personalized balance between information and internal guidance can get thrown out of whack and you can find yourself stuck in ambiguity and doubt. The harder you strain to find the right choice, the more stuck you can get.

Sometimes you get stuck before you've chosen something, and you can't get clear on what to pick. Sometimes the uncertainty and doubt stick around after you've chosen, so the decision stays open and unresolved in your mind and you're filled with dissatisfaction and regret. Either way, you're stuck, and in your bigger, life decisions, you can stay that way for years.

I felt this way about my work for few years until, just a few months ago, I finally made the decision to start my company, Wisdom Soup. Up until then, I'd built a career as a very successful executive coach. I had fantastic clients at the top of some of the largest companies in the world. But a couple years ago, I began to feel like my work was heading in a different direction. I wanted to do work that felt less corporate and more personal. I was drawn to personal transformation and spirituality, which wouldn't really fly with my existing clients.

I gradually developed a pretty good idea of what I wanted my career to become, but I was really dragging my feet on the decision to walk away from the kind of executive coaching I'd been doing. What made this decision particularly hard was that, everywhere I went, it seemed like I ran into people who wanted, more than anything, to be executive coaches. Every plane ride, every event, every party I went to, I would end up talking to or sitting next to someone who was trying to build the career I wanted to step away from. It made me feel guilty and ungrateful. Being an executive coach is objectively a great choice, but I needed to make room in my life to start something new, and the conflict I felt about that kept me in doubt much longer than I needed to be. It overwhelmed my own natural decision process and left me with too much ambiguity. Because I was struggling with doubt, I hung on to the safety of that professional, corporate identity in a way that really slowed me down.

What slowed me down was the ambiguity caused by how other people felt about my decision, but you can experience the same kind of ambiguity any time your decision process gets out of balance. Any time you are listening to too many opinions or reviews, paying too much or too little attention to information, searching for more external confirmation or validation, comparing what you have to other options, or burying yourself in statistics and data, you risk overwhelming your own internal, emotional guidance system with ambiguity. Once you get out of balance and overwhelmed, you start spinning in that circle of doubt, searching for something to make you feel the way you want to feel so that you can make a choice, but the more you look outside yourself, the more ambiguity you have and the more confusing it becomes.

This kind of doubt serves no productive purpose. It's not helping you learn, or grow, or get closer to a solution. If you've ever listened to a vinyl record that's been scratched, you know that the needle will get stuck in that one scratched groove, so the same few words in a song will repeat themselves over and over again without stopping. There's no magic moment where the record spontaneously learns from going in circles and unsticks itself. In the same way, when you're suffering from doubt, spinning in circles, you aren't getting closer to an answer. It's only when you pick up the record player needle and move it that you can finally make progress again. That's why it's so important to identify where your doubt is coming from, so that you can pick up the needle and move on.

Your Doubt Starts in Your Decisions

Most of the time, your doubt starts in your decisions, when you're trying to make the best choice you possibly can. It's often that idea of finding the best choice that gets people in trouble. Most people think about decision making as an effort to figure out which choice is the best one. We focus on the features or attributes of the different options, thinking that there is some quality, or mix of qualities, that one of the options possesses that will make it objectively better than the other options. However, most of the time, there is no one choice that is objectively best for everyone. Most of the options you consider in any choice you make will have both good and bad things about them. The choice that feels best to you might be different from the choice that feels best to someone else.

The feeling of "best" is subjective. The option that you think is flawed and undesirable may seem perfect to someone else. So, if every option has good and bad things about it, how does something become the best choice in your mind? How do you quiet any doubts so that you can fall in love with your choices?

Here's what's really interesting; a choice often becomes the best choice *not* because it's inherently best, but *because of how you choose it*. When it comes to freeing yourself from doubt, the process that you use to make decisions is as important as, and sometimes more important than, the quality of what you choose.

One of the biggest factors that determines how you feel about your choices is the process that you use to make decisions. Your own personal decision process is the key. One of the most important functions of your decision process is to *remove ambiguity from your decisions so that you can feel good about the choices you make.* Your decision process is the *series of steps* you go through to take you from being undecided to being decided. To help make that transition possible, your decision process should help you by removing enough ambiguity that you can feel confident that you have made the best choice you possibly could.

What this means is that, when you are torturing yourself with doubt, cycling in and out of your choices and feeling bad, you may be subconsciously doing something during your decision process that is causing you to feel that way. If you are the one causing your doubt, then that means that you have the power to fix it and get back into flow.

Going Deep

This book is going to help you free yourself from doubt so you can get back into flow, and it's going to do that by making you aware of when and how doubt is taking over your decisions. To be most effective, this can't be a book that just glances across the surface of the issue. We have to go deep. We have to really pick apart and analyze your decision process so that you know it and understand it.

In order to get the whole picture, you'll look at your decisions from a few different vantage points;

In *Part 2*, you'll look very close up, all the way inside your brain, and see the mechanics of how you think when you make decisions. You'll learn about the thinking tools that you use to evaluate and understand your decisions, and how they operate before, during and after you make your choices.

Then in *Part 3*, you'll take a step back and get ready to see the bigger picture by seeing how those thinking tools are applied, using a baseline decision model I'll provide. This will give you something to compare yourself to.

Then comes the fun in *Part 4*, where you look at yourself. You'll use the questions in a simple flow chart to identify your own soul type, you'll read the description of your decision process and you'll see the amazing skills and talents it makes available to you. In this section we'll talk about how doubt is likely to enter your decisions based on your soul type and what you can do about it.

By looking at your decision process from these different vantage points, I'll help you unravel your decision process so that you can see and reduce the doubt in your decisions. I'll show you how you can reduce the doubt you experience according to your own specific decision process so that you can get closer to flow.

But first, we'll finish off this section with chapters 2 and 3, where we'll get clearer about what I mean when I talk about ambiguity. I'll define ambiguity and introduce how it interacts with your decision process.

CHAPTER 2

Amiguity: What You Don't Know Won't Hurt You... Or Will It?

n the last section, I said that one of the most important functions of your decision process is to remove ambiguity from your decisions so that you can feel good about the choices you make. Ambiguity in your decision process is what causes your doubt. Before you understand how to have less of it, we have to get really clear on what ambiguity is and where it shows up in your life. In this section, I'll explain ambiguity.

Worries

My neighbor's little girl loves science. She likes to play a little question game that we call, "what would happen if...?" Most of the time, the questions she asks are combining some bit of science or physics with possible morbid outcomes. "What would happen if someone's finger went into that electrical outlet?" or "What would happen if the earth was swallowed by a black hole?"

Her game is sort of morbidly funny, but it reveals a truthful insight about the human experience: We live in a state of uncertainty. There are so many factors affecting our existence that we aren't aware of or that we don't understand, and it's possible for anyone to be breathing one moment and dead the next. Despite this, my neighbor's questions are never worries for her. They are about unpredictable, unknowable, unlikely things that you couldn't prepare for. So she just asks her questions cheerfully and moves on.

Worries are different. In order to worry about something, it needs to have some decision component for you. The worry comes from feeling some kind of personal responsibility to act or do something in a particular situation when the best path forward isn't clear. It might be a situation where you feel responsible for your own safety, for the safety or well-being of other people, or for work that needs to be done, but you aren't sure what to do, and that causes you to worry. If you are anxious about asteroids colliding with the planet, what you are worried about is not the fact that there are asteroids. You are worried about *what you should do* about those asteroids. Should you be building a bomb shelter, or stocking up on astronaut food, or heading to Las Vegas to live large while you still can? The ambiguity of not knowing what you should do creates doubt, and that's uncomfortable.

Something is ambiguous when the meaning is uncertain, or when the decision about something is unclear, so you aren't sure how you should react or what you should do. For example, if you hear a loud bang nearby, one that sounds like a small explosion, you might not know if it's a gunshot, some fireworks, or a car backfiring. It could mean many things, so the meaning of the sound is ambiguous, and you don't know if you should duck for cover or go about your business.

When something is ambiguous for you, you have a hard time resolving the question, "What does it mean?" And in decisions, you will struggle with the question, "What should I do?"

Generally speaking, ambiguity feels uncomfortable. Ambiguity can make you worry about what bad thing might happen and creates a space in your thoughts which you can fill with imagined fears. It leaves too much room for your imagination to generate problems, and that takes you out of flow.

Ambiguity has at least two levels. One is the *specific* ambiguity you might have about what you decide day to day. The other is the *general* ambiguity you might have about your life's circumstances.

Specific Ambiguity

There's a tradition among the kids in the neighborhood where I live to "Ghost" each other. In the days before Halloween, they will sneak up to each other's door, leave a paper bag full of candy on the door mat, ring the bell and run away. It's a really nice tradition if you understand what's going on. This was all new to me when we moved into the area, and the neighborhood I grew up in wasn't so nice. In my neighborhood, the tradition was to put a paper bag full of dog poop on the door step, light it on fire, ring the bell and run away. Needless to say, the first time my kids were ghosted and we opened the door, I approached that little brown paper bag with caution.

The paper bag on my doorstep was an example of specific ambiguity because it related to an isolated event or decision. I wasn't sure if it was a good present or a bad present, so the meaning and contents of the paper bag were ambiguous, and I wasn't sure if I should open it or not. Specific ambiguity happens in one instance or context, rather than being part of your ongoing life where you would experience more general ambiguity. (If you have an ongoing issue with ambiguous paper bags on your doorstep, you might want to think about a new neighborhood).

Every individual decision is an opportunity for specific ambiguity. You can have specific ambiguity about which sandwich to pick for lunch, or which presidential candidate to vote for. When you feel specific ambiguity about a decision, it means you aren't sure about your choice. You might be unable to decide between the choices you have, or wonder if there is another choice you would like better.

General Ambiguity

General ambiguity, on the other hand, is about big, broader questions in your life that you experience over time. You can experience general ambiguity about any situation or circumstance you find yourself in, whether it's a relationship, a softball team, or a job. I have a friend who spends most of her time in any relationship wondering if she should end the relationship. It's really miserable for her. Her relationships are always just good enough to make it hard to break up, but not happy enough to want to stay. And she ends up in an uncomfortable state of general ambiguity and indecision.

When you experience general ambiguity, it feels like you are stuck in the middle of deciding something indefinitely. Sometimes you think you should stay, and that feeling lasts for a short while, until you begin to think you should go again. You go back and forth, you're in, then you're out, over and over again, feeling dissatisfied about what you're doing or what you've chosen.

The Effects of Ambiguity

Each of us can experience ambiguity differently in our own lives. For me, too much ambiguity can put a haze over any experience. In decisions, it makes it hard to commit to my choice, and it can cloud any decision I make with a feeling of discontent or reluctance.

When you have ambiguity about which choice to make, it's like an empty space that you fill up with your imagination, and for some reason you rarely imagine puppies and rainbows. You worry about all the bad things that could happen because of what you don't know. You worry that you'll feel bad about your choice, or that a better one will come along, or that the one you picked will give you food poisoning. Sometimes you experience ambiguity as regret, which makes you feel bad about yourself as a decision-maker and dissatisfied with whatever you chose.

Such negative thoughts can take a real toll on your happiness. In fact, studies have shown that rumination and worry contribute to mental illnesses such as depression and anxiety.[i] If you focus on ambiguity, the worry it causes can be a distraction that makes it harder to get things done in general and in specific areas of life. In other words, it takes you out of flow.

CHAPTER 3

Your Soul Type And Decision Process

n Chapter 1, I said that one of the biggest factors that determines how you feel about your choices is the process that you use to make decisions. You have a specific decision process that you use that is different from other people. It's the series of steps and behaviors you use to take you from the beginning of a decision to its completion and accomplishment. When it comes to understanding your doubt, your own personal decision process is the key.

You can think about your decision process as a habit because it exists below your awareness and you do it without thinking, except that it has always been there. It isn't something you learned to do last year. You can't remember not being this way. I saw these patterns in my children from their earliest moments. One was determined and bold, and the other was cautious and observant, and they made decisions very differently.

These thinking patterns are like a blueprint that you're born with. It's part of what I call your soul type. It's not modeled or learned in childhood– in fact your soul type and the decision process that comes from it may be completely different from your parents. But it is a definable pattern that we can name and describe.

Since it's always been part of you, you might not see this pattern unless something calls your attention to it. At times you might notice that you make decisions faster or slower than your friend when you're ordering lunch together, or you might notice that your spouse or partner is more or less cautious than you are, but these are just bits and pieces of the pattern and they don't give you the insight and self-knowledge that becomes clearer when you see the whole thing.

When you become aware of your decision process, you can start to notice its strengths and potential weaknesses. You'll be able to recognize when and how doubt is finding its way into your decisions. Once you see this, then just a few adjustments can dramatically reduce the doubt you feel.

Sometimes We Create Ambiguity

Your decision process usually works great for you. It reduces your ambiguity and helps you to make choices you feel confident about. However, during some decisions, your decision process might not work as smoothly. Sometimes the steps involved in your decision process, the *way* that you make your decisions at each step along the way, may itself be creating even more ambiguity for you.

I'm reminded of this every time I look in my closet. I have a dress in my closet that I decided to buy and now I feel terrible about it. It was an impulse purchase and once I got it home I didn't like it as much, so I left the tags on thinking I'd return it, but I didn't get back to the store in time and now it's too late. The longer it hangs there the less I like it. I would feel bad about getting rid of it and I don't like it well enough to give to a friend, so it just sits in my closet looking at me.

When I look at how I made my decision to buy that dress, I can see that I did just about everything wrong. I bought it on impulse, so I skipped steps I would normally take to think it through. I left the tags on and didn't commit to it, then I got stuck re-evaluating it over and over again as it sat there in my closet. There is absolutely nothing wrong with my dress – I liked it well enough to buy it in the first place. I just don't like it anymore. The way I made my decision left me with a lot of doubt about my choice.

How sure do you feel about your decisions? Chances are that some percentage of your decisions don't go well. I don't mean that you are necessarily making bad decisions - in fact your choices are probably great. I mean that you just feel badly about them.

For some number of your decisions (and for some people, this number may be ALL of their decisions), the way you make your decisions leaves you with too much ambiguity and doubt. Maybe for you this means you push ahead in your decisions but end up with buyer's remorse, or maybe you hold back so you miss out on opportunities. Maybe you torture yourself with indecision and burn cycle after cycle without any resolution, and that makes you feel negative and self-critical, dissatisfied and unhappy.

You may be so accustomed to doubt that you just think of it as a natural part of life. You might learn to accept how doubt feels and just move on, trying to do the best you can. It's possible to make decisions every day and still get things done in spite of the fact that you might be experiencing doubt. However, what I'm saying is that when you have too much ambiguity and doubt about your decisions, you might be experiencing a lot less flow than you could be. Even if you make the best choices, you could end up feeling really dissatisfied because your decision process isn't doing what it needs to. It's letting you down.

One of the important functions of your decision process is to *remove ambiguity from your decisions so that you can feel good about the choices you make.* Your decision process is the *series of steps* you go through to take you from being undecided to being decided. To help make that transition possible, your decision process should help you by removing enough ambiguity so that you feel confident that you made the best choice you possibly could.

The good news is that your brain is designed to think about decisions in a way that can give you an amazing capability to reduce ambiguity. Understanding the way you think about decisions will show you where and how you can tweak your decision process so that it is better aligned with this capability in order to take full advantage of it. Once you see how *you* make decisions, not only will you be able to make your decisions more clearly, but you can also see where you can adjust your decision making to improve how you feel about your decisions.

Part Two
The Mechanics of Loving Your Decisions

CHAPTER 4

The Mechanics of Loving Your Decisions

n this book I've been saying that whether or not you've make the best decision is often a matter of opinion. When you feel happy with a decision, it becomes a good decision in your mind, and it helps you feel confident about yourself as a decision-maker. I've also talked about how ambiguity can create doubt about your decisions and get in the way of being in flow. When you reduce your ambiguity, you can move from feeling undecided to feeling great about your decisions.

In this chapter, I'll explain exactly how flow happens in your decisions. It's possible for you to feel less doubt about your decisions more of the time. You have the ability to think about your decisions in a way that not only reduces ambiguity and helps you to choose, but that also reinforces your choices after you've made them and causes you to love them. In other words, there is something about the process that you use to make your decisions that can impact whether or not you fall in love with your choices. To understand and take advantage of this, you need to take a close look at the complex set of interrelated thoughts that happens in your head when you are making decisions.

The Decision Equation

When people talk about making decisions, it's common to focus on the thinking that you do before you choose something. Figuring out what to choose is seen as the critical skill in decision-making, and is thought of as synonymous with decision-making itself.

The period prior to committing is important, but it's only a third of the equation. There are two other periods in decision-making that are equally important, and in some ways, they are more important to being happy and in flow; the actual commitment itself, and the period after committing. This gives us three phases, which are:

Phase 1: Pre-Commitment
Phase 2: Committing to Commitment
Phase 3: Post-Commitment.

In order to understand the thought process that leads to you feeling great about your decisions, I'll explain what happens in your head during each of these three phases, starting with phase 1, which is Pre-Commitment, where two important parts of your brain interact: your emotions and what I call your Difference Engine.

CHAPTER 5

Phase 1: Pre-Commitment

As we have been discussing, our world is full of ambiguity, and none of us have the ability to know everything there is to know about every decision that we make. Even in the best and clearest decisions, there is still going to be an unknown future that we can't predict. This means that, in order to function and get things done in life, you need some way of making reliably good decisions without knowing everything, or in many cases, without knowing much at all about your decisions. Unless you have a psychic hotline on speed dial, trying to reliably make good decisions when you have very little information sounds impossible. How could deciding be anything more than just a guess? And yet, you do it all the time.

The way you think about decisions gives you a remarkable decision-making super power that enables you to make decisions with confidence even when you have just the smallest glimpse of data. As a matter of fact it's so good that, if you were the only one who had it, you could charge a fortune on your own psychic hotline. Fortunately for the rest of us, we all come hard-wired with this amazing capability, and all we have to do is learn to use it effectively.

Your decision making super-power is that you rely on comparison instead of measuring actual values using a neat part of your brain I call your Difference Engine. You aren't measuring things, you are comparing them and seeing their differences.

Your Difference Engine

Your Difference Engine is a part of your brain that helps you to understand and define things. It does this by *putting the thing you seek to understand in relation to something else and observing what is similar and what is different in the comparison.* If you are travelling in a new country and someone serves you a mysterious stew, you might try to understand what it is by comparing it to something you already know. Maybe the stew smells fishy, so it might be similar to a fish stew you once had. Maybe it has potato in it, so it might be similar to a chowder.

Comparison is the method we use to make sense of the world around us. We define things by understanding what they are similar to and what they are not. We create categories of things that are similar in order to understand them better. We know that poodles and terriers both belong to the category called dogs, so they are similar to each other, and it means that they are different from cats and fish. So we define and understand things with our Difference Engine, which tells us what things are similar to and what they are different from.

When you are making decisions, you need to define and understand your options before you can figure out which choice you like best. This is where your Difference Engine is in charge. It will serve up comparisons among your options and point out the differences between them. It enables you to see the benefits of one option in comparison to the benefits of another so that you can determine which one you like better.

Using Your Difference Engine to Compare Choices

Using your Difference Engine to make comparisons is how you figure out what you like. Without something to compare a particular option to, it's much harder to figure out whether that option is a good or bad one. I experienced this early in my career when I worked at Microsoft. I had to hire a marketing firm to produce collateral for a new program we were launching. Even though our company had a whole list of approved vendors, they only sent me one marketing firm to consider. I hadn't worked with a marketing firm before, so I had no experience and nothing to compare them to.

Trying to decide whether or not to work with the one marketing firm I was given to consider was hard. I had to try and evaluate the merits of that firm's portfolio based on whether their material looked cool to my (very) untrained eye. To make a reliably good decision, I would've needed to know a lot about marketing materials, and I didn't. I had no idea what I was looking for, and really couldn't tell whether what that one marketing firm was showing me was good or not. I had nothing to compare that firm's work to.

Later in my life I ran into the same sort of situation. I needed to select a firm to design marketing materials for another launch. But this time it was a completely different experience. This time I interviewed three companies instead of just one, so when

I looked at their work, I could compare them to each other. It became wonderfully clear which ones were good and which ones compared less favorably, and I felt very confident about my final choice.

When you use comparison, you don't have to know everything about a decision and you don't have to be a subject matter expert. You just have to look for the differences between or among two or more things. Rather than asking, "Is this one good?" which requires that you have knowledge and expertise to judge the merit of something, you are now asking, "Which of these two things is better?"

When you use comparison, you can look and find observable differences that don't necessarily require expertise. As long as you are comparing two similar things, this means you can evaluate options you know very little about with relatively high accuracy. You can make reliably good decisions when you don't have all the information. You can act without knowing all the possible outcomes. Using comparison to make a decision is thus a dramatically smaller challenge with significantly less ambiguity.

If you had to wait until you were 100% certain about all aspects of a decision, you'd never get anything done because you wouldn't be able to resolve the ambiguity. In using comparison to make a choice, you have a way of making *predictably good choices with just the smallest amount of information* – and this is incredibly efficient.

What You Choose for Comparison

Your Difference Engine can make your decision making more efficient, even easier for you. The really hard part is that first you have to find something to compare to. Sometimes the comparison is really obvious. If you are trying to pick between two jars of jellybeans, you compare them to each other. In other cases, there might not be an obvious comparison, and you will have to decide what is most similar about your experience of the things you are evaluating. *What you chose to compare something against can have a dramatic effect on how you perceive it.*

A company in Fort Lauderdale, Florida learned this when it tried to launch a new line of bottled water. The company wanted customers to compare their water to Perrier, and they gave it a premium price. The problem was that their water was for pets. They made Thirsty Dog and Thirsty Cat bottled water. The water had electrolytes and vitamins and came in Crispy Beef or Tangy Fish flavor. Most of us have a hard time keeping our pets from drinking out of the toilet, which makes toilet water a much more logical comparison than Perrier. It's not surprising that people were unwilling to pay $1.79 for Thirsty Dog water when toilet water is such a treat and is available for free. Thirsty Dog and Thirsty Cat are now listed among the greatest all time product flops.

Using your Difference Engine optimally is sophisticated work. If your Difference Engine chooses the wrong thing for comparison, it can lead you to make incorrect assumptions and mistakes. For example, there was a Labradoodle in Virginia that had an unusual haircut. And when he was playing outside near the city zoo, his haircut caused a flurry of 911 calls. Charles the Labradoodle looked an awful lot like a lion (although he had no interest in eating people).

Choosing something for comparison that doesn't fit can cause you to misunderstand things and react in a way that is inappropriate or not in your best interest. Through rich life experience, we can draw upon a range of comparisons in making our decisions. In life, we develop memories and judgement that makes us better and better at using our Difference Engine. This is because we develop so much to work with and compare to when decision making.

You Feel Your Way to a Decision

Sometimes comparison is quantitative, which makes it pretty straight forward. It can be as simple as a binary choice between more or less, faster or slower. If you are choosing between a bag with 3 apples and another bag with 4 apples simply to get the most apples, all you have to do is count the apples in each bag to get your answer.

But often, decisions are much more subjective, which means that the benefits of the differences between the alternatives are a matter of opinion. In a choice between eating an apple and an orange, the decision would be subjective because both fruits have their own unique benefits and one isn't inherently better than the other. What's tricky about subjective decisions is that there usually isn't one "right" answer, and it's up to you to decide if you like one more than another based on how you feel about those differences. Maybe today you are in the mood for an apple, so in this case, the apple becomes the right decision. Generally, subjective decisions can be a lot harder because, when subjective opinion is involved, it's harder to resolve the ambiguity you might have about a choice. When there is no clear answer, there is no clear answer.

Luckily for you, subjective decision making comes naturally to you. In fact, it's what you're built for. You don't actually think about whether or not you *like* a decision – you feel your way there. For every single decision you make, the moment of choosing starts with your emotions and is based on how you feel. If you watched your brain activity during decision making, you would clearly see the area of the brain dealing with subconscious emotions light up first, followed closely by the rational, more conscious region. Your subconscious emotions decide how they feel about the decision, and then your conscious mind rationalizes the choice.

I'm not saying that you don't think at all before you make a decision. Your Difference Engine thinks constantly. But for every comparison your Difference Engine is making, your emotions are involved. It's actually your emotions that are making the call as to which one choice is better. Your emotions decide. Your Difference Engine does some of the work but the real decision is there on the gut subconscious level, first.

Whether or not we realize this, we rely on our emotions to make decisions. The emotion-centered portion of your brain is essential to your decision making. This portion of your brain is so essential that if it is damaged or non-functional, you will be completely stuck, and unable to decide anything at all. Neuroscientist Antonio Damasio studied people who had damaged the portion of their brains that generate emotions. He found that, while those people could understand the logic of a decision and could weigh both sides (using their Difference Engines), when it came to actually deciding, they simply couldn't choose. Without emotions, they didn't know which choice was better so they didn't know which one to pick.

Your Personal Emotional Context

Whether or not you like something can be impacted by the context you experience it in. If you experience a new city on a beautiful sunny day, it can cause you to feel more positively about the city. On the other hand, when you're in an environment you don't like, your perception of what you experience in that environment is negatively impacted. For example, eating great cake in a garbage dump is not the same as eating that same great cake in a wonderful bakery. Another example: if you associate something even as nice as great cake with an emotion of sadness, the thing or cake itself becomes sad in your mind. This is because sadness is your personal, *emotional context* for experiencing that cake.

During the dot.com bust in Silicon Valley, layoffs were a common thing. But they were always sad. In the middle of it, I began working with a client company that had let so many people go that it had unfilled space. So the company moved all the remaining employees down to one end of the building and left the other half of the building vacant and dark. The problem was that the only coffee maker was in the kitchen at the vacant end of the building, so to get coffee you had to walk past all the empty cubicles.

When the company was busy and growing, that walk would've been a chance to see friends and to feel the energy of productivity all around you. It would've been fun to go get coffee. But after the layoffs, that walk to the kitchen became interminably long, and it felt spooky and sad. And the floor of that hallway was linoleum, so every step you took reverberated and echoed back to you from the sea of silent, dark cubicles. (Really, who wants coffee that badly?)

The point is, the coffee they were serving never changed, and there is nothing inherently sad about an empty cubicle, but my perception of going to get coffee changed when it took on the context of all those people losing their jobs. It became sad coffee. If someone else walked down that hallway who knew nothing about the layoffs, and maybe thought the company was growing instead of shrinking, getting coffee would've felt very different to that person. Sadness was my personal, emotional context through which I perceived and understood the experience of going for coffee.

It's all about what you associate with your experience. Your positive or negative associations can impact just about everything you see, think, feel, and know. Association itself can impact your understanding of things that would generally be considered objective, quantitative and measurable, such as simple questions of more or less, and longer or shorter. I find this is especially true in my experience of time. I recently had to get my driver's license renewed, so I blocked a few hours off on my calendar and mentally prepared myself to be very, very bored. Time passes very slowly at the DMV.

Of course, the truth is that time always passes at the same rate. We know this because we have watches to measure time. But our *experience* of time doesn't work that simply. Time spent in line at the DMV always takes much longer than time spent dining with friends. Even though the actual measure of each hour is always 60 minutes, without the aid of a watch, we would be terrible at estimating time. We evaluate the length of an hour based on whether we liked that hour or not. Fun hours seem to have fewer minutes in them and are much shorter than boring hours. DMV-waiting hours have hundreds of minutes in them. If you feel bored at the DMV, then DMV minutes become long and boring.

So, your experience of something can affect your experience of making decisions about it or something related to it. When you are making decisions by evaluating whether or not you like something, your emotions carry all of your past experiences and understandings into your experience of each of your alternatives. Every choice you make is deeply personal because you bring the *emotional context of your own life experience* to every decision that you make. If your context around an alternative is positive, you feel positive about making your choice. Someone else may attach a totally different meaning to that alternative and may not like your choice. But your *positive emotional context* makes it the right choice for you.

The Nature of Emotions

There is an evolutionary reason for your emotion-centered brain-circuitry. Emotions are fast. When you are in immediate danger because an angry bear is chasing you, you can't spend a lot of time thinking. Your emotions don't rely on thinking at all. They don't evaluate the relative size and ferocity of the angry bear, weigh the pros and cons of playing dead, or spend time considering which tree is better to climb. Emotions simply respond to danger by feeling scared, and make you run or climb to safety. Emotions are much faster than cognitions, and when survival is an issue, speed matters.

When you make decisions, you need your emotions to feel your way to the best choice, but your emotions are unruly and hard to control. They are very sensitive to danger, and there can be a lot of perceived danger in decision making. You aren't able to know everything and you have to make choices using your best judgement with a limited amount of information. It's the ambiguity that can make decision-making scary, and it can make you fearful. You have learned that unexpected things happen. When you hear stories about mistakes, failures and regrets, those scenes live large in your imagination. You imagine all the negative outcomes that could happen from whatever decision you make and the fear you feel can keep your emotions running for safety instead of doing what you need them to – making a decision.

You have to deal with ambiguity and fear in order to tame your emotions so that you can make decisions and get work done in life. *This is why your Difference Engine is so important.* It can take a really ambiguous and scary decision and help you boil it down to something simpler – a comparison between two things you know. When you reduce the ambiguity in the decision, you reduce your fear, so your emotions can relax and do what you need them to do - quickly assess how you feel and commit to a choice.

Shifting Your Difference Engine

There is a myth about Midas, the King of Lydia, who wished for the power to turn everything he touched into gold. He was thrilled when he got this amazing super-power, but when he accidently turned his daughter to gold he realized that he had too much of a good thing.

You might sometimes feel the same way about your Difference Engine. Your Difference Engine isn't self-regulating. It doesn't know when you'd like it to stop, and it never stops itself. Your Difference Engine is always on, scanning your environment for alternatives and comparing differences, seeing which option is better. Your Difference Engine will make you think about how your neighbor's house compares to yours, or how your clothes fit compared to the last time you put them on, or how the weather this year compares to spring of last year. Your Difference Engine will ask you, which is better or worse?

Imagine you've done all the work to come to a decision, and that you are feeling very happy and satisfied with your choice. Then imagine that, after all that work making your decision, your Difference Engine shows up at the door with a new batch of alternatives to show you. This situation would feel quite counterproductive. Looking at more choices after you have made your decision would introduce ambiguity into the choice you have already made. This could only make you feel doubts about your decision.

Once you become aware of your Difference Engine, it can feel a little like a dog with a tennis ball he wants you to throw over and over again. Every time you start to relax, that slobbery ball is dropped in your lap again. Your Difference Engine is like the dog who wants you to throw the ball again, asking, "how about this one, better or worse?" If you've already made your choice, this can be annoying.

You can never stop your Difference Engine. So how do you prevent your Difference Engine from showing you new alternatives and comparisons after you're ready to commit? The answer is to shift it into a new gear. This critical step happens when you make a *commitment to your choice*.

CHAPTER 6

Phase 2: Committing to Commitment

> "In any moment of decision the best thing you can
> do is the right thing, the next best thing is the wrong
> thing, and the worst thing you can do is nothing."
>
> **THEODORE ROOSEVELT**

Roosevelt's quote is true on several levels. On the surface, it means that the point of making a decision is to create change or action, and the value of that forward momentum outweighs even the risk of picking the wrong path. After all, even the wrong path at least teaches you something about the right path, which can help you get somewhere in the long run.

But what I really like about Roosevelt's quote is that it emphasizes the central importance and pivotal nature of the moment of decision. All action, momentum, learning and developments come from the moment of decision. If life was run from the cockpit of an airplane, there would be a big red button labeled "decision" and it would be the button that started the engines and made the whole thing go.

The problem is that there is a lack of clarity about what counts has having competed a decision. For my purposes, and to help you move from doubt to flow, what really counts is when you make a true commitment.

Making a decision and making a commitment are not the same thing. It's possible to make a decision, and not be committed to that decision. Making a decision can be anything from handing over your credit card, signing a contract, or turning left instead of right. It's an action step, so it feels like you're finished with the thinking part. The truth is that the decision isn't complete, but in some of your decisions, this may be as far as you go. Stopping after this first action step gives you some of the benefits of making a decision without having to really be committed. You have a way out if it turns out you made a mistake. You can always take it back. Leaving yourself an exit may make you feel prudent, planning ahead, just in case your decision goes south. The elements of that plan can be anything from money you set aside for a rainy day, a person or relationship that you would fall back on, or the fat pants you keep in your closet in case the diet doesn't work. These elements seem innocuous, except that you know in your mind that they are part of your exit plan.

When movie actors filmed bedroom scenes back in the 1930's they had to comply with the Motion Picture Production Code, also known as the Hays Code. It required that the actors were not allowed to get fully into bed together. They always had to keep one foot on the ground. This ensured that there was no hanky panky. Keeping your alternatives around and a back door open after you've made your choice is like keeping one foot on the ground. It prevents any serious commitment from happening. If you have a way out, that means you are not all the way "in", and you can't get emotionally invested in your choice. You wouldn't put your money into a piggy bank unless you were certain that the piggy was yours and you could keep it. In the same way, you won't invest your identity or your sense of self into a choice unless you feel like you own it and can't give it up. Having an out is a way of protecting yourself emotionally by keeping distance from your choices and not getting attached to them.

When you fail to become emotionally invested in your choices, you end up teetering on the edge of commitment, trying to keep your balance. Instead of looking across the canyon and jumping to happiness, you end up looking down into what feels like certain death. The longer you look at it, the scarier it becomes. The fear of falling to your commitment-death becomes the focus.

To avoid this fear you will start to look for ways to justify backing down from the edge of your commitment. Your Difference Engine kicks in, comparing the risk of jumping to the perceived safety of not jumping. Your Difference Engine will look for reasons not to jump, not to commit.

This means you will be working hard to find reasons not to like the choice you made. Instead of having to forgive your partner for leaving their socks on the floor and chewing with their mouth open, it's easy to consider backing out at every little offense. You've already got an exit plan. You have to be willing to take the risk of being hurt or disappointed and get fully into bed with your choices or you will only see what is wrong with everything you chose and open yourself up to doubt.

It's Easy to Have Doubts

Falling in love with your choice isn't something to take for granted – it's not a given thing. It's really easy to have doubts. There is no single right way of succeeding in life. There is usually more than one good option in any decision you make. Who knows what would have happened if you hadn't left your last company when you did, or if you'd gone to school somewhere else, or if you'd bought that other house you liked? That other life you would've had is like a parallel universe of things that could have been but aren't. In that life you would have different friends, maybe be part of a weekend softball league, and you would've taken up scuba diving or clogging. It's hard to say which life would've been better – they are probably each good in different ways, and that's a little disturbing.

But here's something we do know – after that one decision came lots of other decisions. Every step you've taken has been the result of some new decision. Each one helped to create and add definition to the life you have now. You are a good decision maker, and if you have faith in that, then you can have faith that your life is directionally best. In other words, you are making decisions to set the direction of your life, and each individual choice matters less than the cumulative effect of being a good decision maker over time. You may take a few detours now and then, but overall you are getting where you want to go.

This works great as long as you trust your ability to make good choices. But what if you don't? What if you second-guess yourself, or feel regret about your choices? If you're in doubt about the direction your life is going, you are going to make choices that aren't aligned with that direction – that maybe pull you in new directions. This is fine if you do it once in a while, but if you do it all the time, you are always pulled in different directions and you are wasting your energy half-pursuing a life you're not sure if you want. This explains why moving from doubt to flow is so powerful. When you're in flow, your energy is much more focused so there is a lot more momentum to your progress.

What Makes a Commitment

The most important thing about commitment is that, in order for it to be accomplished successfully, three things have to happen.

1. **Make a decision** – Making a decision is the moment of choosing, when you have distinguished which of your options you like best and are ready to move forward. Making a decision sometimes includes an action step, such as handing over your credit card or turning left instead of right.

2. **Give up the alternatives** – The idea behind giving up your alternatives is that you want to be able to stop thinking about your alternatives. In order to stop your Difference Engine from thinking about your alternatives or about other, new options, you need to create a mental and physical separation between you and other choices. Whatever you considered as another option, or whatever might tempt you as a replacement for your decision, should be given away, pushed away, or otherwise kept out of your reach. Ideally, you want to make sure that those other options are no longer available to you. This could mean you let other offers expire, throw away the catalogues and stop shopping, give your leads to someone else, or proactively announce both your disinterest in other options and your commitment to your choice.

3. **Burn your bridges** – There is a story in Burmese history about the Battle of Naung Yo in 1540. The Burmese Prince, Bayinnaung, faced a superior force of Mons on the other side of a river. After crossing the river, Bayinnaung ordered the pontoon bridge they crossed to be destroyed. He wanted to provide a clear signal to his troops that there would be no retreat so that they would have no choice but to fully commit themselves to fighting. When you burn your bridges, you eliminate any opportunities you might have had to back out, retrace your steps, or undo your decision. This means take the tags off, don't negotiate an easy out for yourself, and tear up your little black book.

It is number two and three on the list above that we have difficulty with. In order for a decision to be complete, you have to give up all the alternatives and burn your bridges. You have to decide if you are in or you are out. No return policies, no back-up plans, no cherished hopes, no back doors, and no regrets about the one-that-got-away.

This may seem rash and impractical, particularly for consequential life decisions. We live in an era of prenuptial agreements. But consider this. If you make a decision without burning your bridges, your Difference Engine will continue to compare your choice to other options. This will make you under appreciate and feel less satisfied with what you have. Since you have less on the line, you might not try as hard to make your choice work for you. Your dissatisfaction makes it harder for your choice to succeed, and you could end up back at square one, having to go through the decision process all over again.

One example of the risks of not fully committing is a finding by the National Center for Family and Marriage showing that married couples who do not pool their income are 145 percent more likely to end up in divorce court, compared to couples who share a bank account.[ii] Now, whether or not this pooled income in marriage example works for you, the point is that if you only half commit to any choice, there is a greater chance that your decision will be unsuccessful or leave you dissatisfied. The more consequential the decision is, the bigger a life choice that decision is, the more disruptive a lack of commitment to it will be, and the unhappier the not fully committed to decision will make you.

Real Commitment

Making a real commitment, which includes taking a leap of faith, giving up the alternatives, and burning your bridges, is like flipping a switch. It changes the function of your Difference Engine so that it stops comparing. Instead, it starts helping you to see what's best about the choice you made, and it helps you to get emotionally invested in it. This helps all the other options you left behind to lose their appeal so that you can focus all your energy in one positive direction. Your ambiguity is reduced, which makes you feel more confident in yourself as a decision-maker. When you commit to the decisions you make in life, it helps you move from doubt to flow, where you'll have a better, happier and more satisfied life.

The mechanics of how this happens still rely on your Difference Engine and your emotions, but now they are each functioning differently.

CHAPTER 7

Phase 3: Post-Commitment

B efore you make a commitment to the decision you are making, your Difference Engine is objective. It looks for any comparative information it can find to help you make your choice. Then you make your decision. You make a commitment to making this decision, giving up all the alternatives and burning your bridges.

It's at this point that something changes, and your Difference Engine starts to behave differently. Your Difference Engine is no longer objective. Rather than looking objectively at all available information, your Difference Engine now selectively and subjectively searches for and processes only good news about your decision.

The Difference Engine Sets it Apart

Neuroscientists have found that your Difference Engine uses two different regions in your brain for processing information about the decisions you've made. One region is for good news about your decision and the other region is for bad news about your decision. The region that processes good news works great. If you hear a sports commentator predicting the victory of the team you love, you will absorb every word and it will make you feel happy.

On the other hand, if the commentator sitting next to him disagrees and explains why he thinks your favorite team will lose; chances are you will simply not retain this less than desirable information. The region for processing bad news about your choices doesn't work very well. An MRI of this brain activity shows up as just a tiny little flicker. In her book, *The Optimism Bias*, Tail Sharot calls this the "Selective Update Failure." We just don't hear as much of what we don't want to hear. If you have ever asked a child to stop what he or she is doing and help with some chore, you have a vivid image of what this looks like. It is apparent that the child can hear you, but he or she is unresponsive. Words go in, and nothing happens.

Not only does your Difference Engine practice this selective listening to filter out any negative information about your choice, but it also proactively searches for new, positive information that supports your choices. Instead of asking "which one is better?" like it did before you committed to your choice, it now asks, "What is better about the one you have?" It will dwell on the benefits you respond to most, look for new advantages that you hadn't thought of before, and seek social support or agreement from other people.

I put my Difference Engine to work when I got a fantastic new blender that cost much more than a blender should. This encouraged me to develop a strong attachment to my blender. I ran to the store and bought leeks and asparagus and every other kind of blend-able vegetable. I made blended soups every day, sometimes twice a day, for months. My family was somewhat enthusiastic at first, but gradually hinted and then insisted that they were getting tired of soup, so I made soup for friends. I was soup-obsessed. My house always smelled like onions. I was thrilled with how easy and healthy it was to eat vegetables in soup. My family compromised and grew accustomed to blended fruit smoothies, so everyone was happy. This was my Difference Engine in action, helping me to feel great about spending so much on a blender. By the way, my blender really is that awesome.

This is where we historically have gotten confused about doubt in our decisions. It's natural to see how much I enjoy my blender and think that I was lucky to have made the right choice. The truth is that I could have bought a griddle or a popcorn maker or any other small appliance and it would've had an equal chance at making me happy. It's my decision to buy the appliance that I am happy about. I feel good about making a good decision. To support and reinforce my decision to buy the expensive blender, I searched for new uses and I involved other people who would enjoy my soup. That is my Difference Engine in action, eliminating doubt by helping me to find more reasons why my decision was a great idea.

Emotions Get Invested

For many people, buying a house is one of the most stressful decisions that they will make. The amazing thing is that we are all fantastic at buying houses. No matter which house you purchase, it will probably turn out to be the right house in the long run. This isn't because we have highly evolved nesting instincts that mysteriously guide us to the perfect rambler. It's because once we own something, we feel differently about it. We like it more. This is called the *endowment effect.*[iii] People like their own houses so much that they tend to value them much higher than other people do. When a homeowner tries to price and sell his own home without the help of an agent, that homeowner sets an asking price that is an average of 10% to 20% above the market.

Homeowners are great examples of this endowment effect. In their minds, their homes are better than the other comparable homes in their neighborhoods. They will point out the pretty chandelier they installed and the new closet organizers they added. But in truth the perceived difference is due entirely to the fact that it is theirs.

When you drive a rental car, do you take it through a car wash before returning it? How about getting the oil checked? Not likely. On the contrary, you would probably not think twice about parking it in a compact spot between two giant, door-dinging SUVs while your kids fingerpaint with powdered donuts in the back seat. Things that we own get a much higher standard of care.

We Own Our Decisions

In the same way that we own our cars and our houses, we also own our decisions. After you commit to a choice, and that choice becomes yours, your subconscious decides that it likes the one you chose more than the others. Whatever you didn't choose becomes less appealing. Think about the close run contest on the first season of American Idol. Kelly Clarkson beat Justin Guarini by a mere 16%. It was a tidy win, but not a landslide. Now you may be asking yourself, Justin who? I had to look up his last name. In 2002, he was so present in the hearts and minds of Americans that 6.3 million people paid money to vote for him via text message. In the end, we decided to go with Kelly. Now we like her much, much more and Justin has faded from our spotlight. We even gave Kelly a few Grammy awards, and we feel better and better about the decision with each new song of hers that we buy. Poor Justin. This process may have been hard on him, but this is a very good thing for your happiness. You feel good about what you decided.

The degree of ownership you feel in your decision depends upon how much of an investment you make in that choice. When you make an investment in a decision, it becomes personal because you put something of yourself into it. It is somehow linked to you and your self-image. Some decisions are personal because they have a large impact on your life, such as your choice of career. But even the smallest decisions have the potential to become personal if you are invested in them in some way. General Mills figured this out when they introduced a Betty Crocker cake mix that was complete in the box – all the customer had to do was to just add water. But sales were unexpectedly terrible. After some careful thought, General Mills changed the mix so that bakers had to add water and eggs. This made the customers feel like they were really baking, so they liked the product much better. The new, add-eggs Betty Crocker cake mix was a huge success because it allowed customers to invest their time (and their eggs) in the product. It became more personal. Things can become personal when we invest time or resources in them, when they provide self expression, or when they have a significant impact on our lives.

When you invest in your decision, you are infusing it with a little bit of yourself. When you look at a decision you have invested in, it is no longer just a cake or a car or a house. It is a reflection of you. This can make you like it more, which can make you feel like you made a good choice. Then you feel satisfied, content, and clever for picking the right thing. It makes you feel happy. When you pick a puppy from a new litter, you have little insight as to which one is really going to be the best dog. Once you pick and you commit to a puppy, the puppy will appear cuter or smarter or more special than all those other puppies, and you will feel lucky in your choice. This is not to say that you won't be mad when the puppy pees on your carpet, but, whatever that puppy's flaws, you will see its strengths more easily than anyone else.

Love Happens

Where it can, as often as it can, your brain applies its process of validating your decisions for you, telling you that you have decided on a good choice. This is how your brain creates satisfaction instead of doubt. It tells you that you have made a good choice. However, this freedom from doubt occurs only after you have made a *commitment* to your choice, after you have permanently given up all the alternatives, burned your bridges.

Making a commitment is like throwing a switch in your brain, causing the emotions and the Difference Engine to switch gears and behave differently. It is the behavior of your emotions and your Difference Engine *after* you make a commitment that generates satisfaction. If you never give up your alternatives and burn your bridges, the decision is never completed and satisfaction isn't created. What you have instead is a big pile of increasing doubt as the emotions and the Difference Engine become increasingly unable to set the alternatives apart.

Once you commit, your emotions can get invested in your choice. Your Difference Engine *validates the decision* by enlarging the difference between the choice you made and the choices you rejected. Your Difference Engine is still working to establish the difference between things (the way it did before you committed), but now it is selectively searching only for differences that make your choice look better. Your Difference Engine will even go so far as to pick over the available data, select those facts that support your choice, and brush any negative information aside. Because you now own the choice you made, you will feel that its benefits are more important and more valuable than the benefits of the choice you rejected.

The Power of Being Committed is Strong

The power of being committed to your choices is so strong that it can work to protect your happiness and make you more resilient when bad things happen. You are better able to cope with and process the ambiguity of new, negative information. If bad news becomes apparent, your emotions and your Difference Engine will gradually begin working to change how you feel about the new information to reduce its impact on your happiness. Your Difference Engine acts like a self-righting sailboat, built with an especially buoyant hull so that if it capsizes, it slowly rolls right back up again. This is as great a feature for sailboats as it is for happiness.

I was on my way to a client's office in India when news came that the CEO had unexpectedly left the company. The resulting instability would put the existence of the Indian office at risk. And it was my job to facilitate a full day meeting for the entire office on the day that they would all hear and react to the news. No one ever said consulting is easy.

For the first hour or two, it was an open dialogue. Members of the management team and the more vocal employees compared information, asked questions, made speculations, and generally tried to sort things out while the others listened. One manager was quick to point out the value that the India office provides and began to describe the ways in which India was critical to the mission of the company. He thought the company couldn't afford to close them down. They discussed the newly appointed interim CEO, who they all knew, and after some consideration began to think that he might be pretty good. They took turns describing reasons why he might be good, looking to each other for agreement and confirmation. They speculated that the unexpected change could have had nothing to do with India at all, and perhaps they could continue business as usual. They also discussed less popular half-measures, such as the possibility of additional layoffs.

We took a break mid-morning, and I overheard a few of the quieter employees discussing the hot job market in India. If things at the company went bad, they'd be just fine. You could almost see the capsized boat rolling back, right side up. Their Difference Engines and their emotions were hard at work, trying to make them feel better about the new information. They looked at it from new angles, explained it away, sought confirmation from each other, explored half-measures, and if those measures somehow didn't work, they decided they would not care.

Optimism and Resilience

The natural optimism and resilience that can come from your decision process helps you make the best of things when decisions go badly. This optimism and resilience is so powerful that it can help you cope with the most stressful of life events so that you can pick yourself back up and try again.

British novelist Martin Amis lost his closest friend of 40 years – the only friend with whom he felt he could be emotionally naked. In an interview, he explained that in some ways, his friend's death had left him better off, because "the death of a friend increases your love of life. You treasure the moments on their behalf."

CHAPTER 8

Understanding Your Own Decision Process

Understanding the concepts behind falling in love with your decisions is an important first step. Now we need to apply those concepts to how you make decisions in real life. To make these ideas practical, I will break down the ideas behind falling in love with your decision that we explored in this chapter and apply them to a step-by-step description of a decision making process. The goal is to see how you are taking advantage of, or missing out on using, these skills to reduce ambiguity and feel more satisfaction in your own decision making process.

Something to Compare to

I found that the easiest way to see your own decision style is, of course, to use your Difference Engine to compare it to someone else's. It's only when you look at what other people do that you can start to see how your way is different. To give you something to compare yourself to, I will start you off in the following chapter with an easy to follow explanation of a general *Baseline Decision Style* I have set forth for this book. This is how decisions are described in textbooks and how they might be made by a team or group of people following a set decision making process.

None of us make decisions like this when we are on our own. We all vary from this methodical, baseline approach in some way – we all have some slight deviation. And that's a really good thing. By not conforming completely to a prescribed, scripted process outlining the way you should make decisions, you can bring in your own personal approach to making decisions, to solving particular kinds of problems. When you identify your soul type and decision process later in this book, you'll see that the way you make decisions gives you some remarkable and very useful abilities. You will want to do everything you can to develop these.

By defining your soul type, you can get clarity about your unique skills and abilities so that you can focus on bringing them to your life's work in a way that is meaningful, and it will show you how to balance your decision process to reduce the ambiguity that causes your doubt. Your decision process is the common thread through all of the work that you do. It's the one thing that you can focus on that will impact all the others. When you use your skills most effectively, you will be firing on all cylinders, grabbing life by the lapels and smelling all the roses – in other words, you will be in flow.

Part Three
Baseline Decision Model

CHAPTER 9

The Baseline Decision Making Process

n the last section I described the mechanics of loving your decisions. Now I will make this more practical by breaking those ideas down into stages so that you can see how this thinking occurs during the process of decision making.

For this explanation, I'm using my baseline decision style which will provide a framework for the discussion. This is a general sort of one size fits all decision making description. I'll describe all the steps involved in this baseline decision making process and show how the concepts behind loving your decisions unfold in each step. Then, in the following chapters, you can compare this baseline to your own decision process and see how yours is different. This will help you clarify your own process. This will also show you where the ambiguity might be creeping into your decisions.

The Baseline Decision Style

In order to create a Baseline Decision Making Style that you can use for comparison, I have summarized basic decision making into FOUR stages. I have adapted these stages from the four phases of B. Aubrey Fisher's Decision Emergence Theory.[iv] Fisher defined four phases of decision making: orientation, conflict, emergence, and reinforcement. To develop my Baseline Decision Making Process for the purposes of this book, I am applying these four basic phases, or what I am calling *stages*, to what is going on in the individual's mind while making decisions.

To help explain what this Baseline Decision Making Process looks like, I've pictured it below. Think of each decision you make as a sort of ski jump composed of these four basic stages you see pictured here: Stage 1: Orientation; Stage 2: Comparison; Stage 3: Emergence; and Stage 4: Reinforcement.

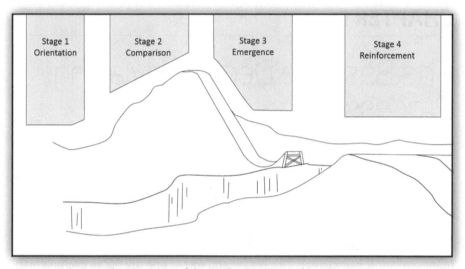

Stage 1
Orientation

Stage 2
Comparison

Stage 3
Emergence

Stage 4
Reinforcement

The Four Stages of the Baseline Decision Making Process

There is specific work that gets done in each of these stages that sets you up to feel satisfied and minimize doubt about your decisions. In order to understand your own decision process it will help to understand exactly what is happening in each stage.

Note that in the following stage descriptions, I refer to the decision maker as a she. Of course this can be either a he or a she.

Stage 1: Orientation

1. **STAGE 1, DEFINED**
    The decision maker starts out thinking through the problem, sees what she wants to accomplish when making a decision about this problem, and searches for possible solutions to this problem. This is Stage 1, the Orientation Stage.

2. **STAGE 1, DESCRIBED**
    Stage 1 is where the decision maker gets clear on what her decision is about. The decision maker tries to understand the problem, thinks through what needs to be accomplished, and thinks about what success might look like. Then the decision maker works to define her priorities and searches for possible alternatives and solutions. This phase includes clarifying what the choices are, tentatively expressing attitudes about the choices, and beginning to form opinions about what decision to make.

3. **STAGE 1, EXAMPLE**
    To give you an example of what happens in each stage of this baseline model, I will use an imagined scenario about a made-up person named Mary, who is going to buy a car. In Stage 1, using this baseline model to make this decision, Mary is becoming aware of the problem or call to action. Her current car is starting to have mechanical problems, and she's also worried about winter conditions because her current car doesn't perform well in snow. As Mary begins to orient to the decision regarding which car to buy, she starts noticing specific cars on the road, and become aware of which ones are appealing. By increasing her awareness of some possible choices, Mary develops clarity around the problem she is trying to solve and what potential solutions might look like.

    Mary will begin to think through the initial parameters of her decision, such as her budget, and how many passengers the car should accommodate. As her awareness of other cars increases, she might start to develop a list of other options that might be important, such as all-wheel-drive.

4. **HOW STAGE 1 LEADS TO THE NEXT STAGE**
    Once a decision maker has become oriented to her decision, she will have a preliminary sense of what she wants. The orienting work done in in Stage 1

provides the initial parameters to guide the search for information and possible solutions in the next stages of the decision.

Stage 2: Comparison

1. **STAGE 2, DEFINED**

   Next, the decision maker moves to Stage 2, the Comparison Stage. This stage may be more challenging as it includes the rather demanding and uphill work of researching, thinking through, and actually comparing all the options.

2. **STAGE 2, DESCRIBED**

   Stage 2 is where the decision maker looks for and evaluates her options. This is a two fold process as there are two parts of the brain that work together in Stage 2. These are the two areas of the brain I discussed earlier, one being *emotions* and the other being the *Difference Engine*. While the Difference Engine is finding and comparing various options, weighing these alternatives, the emotions are also at work. It is the emotions that are *weighing by feeling the value* of each comparison to decide how they, these emotions themselves, feel about each choice.

   Comparing and valuing the alternatives helps the decision maker arrive at a more defined sense of the specific attributes of each choice. As this is taking place, the decision maker is determining what is important to her. As this stage progresses, the decision maker may narrow her search down to a few top options.

3. **STAGE 2, EXAMPLE**

   I will continue our example with Mary and her car from Stage 1, still applying this baseline model. In Stage 2, Mary begins to actively explore the options based on the initial parameters she set in Stage 1. For example, in Stage 1, Mary determined that she is in the market for a five passenger car with all-wheel-drive, and that she is working with a mid-range budget. Now in Stage 2, Mary goes to car dealers and searches used cars online and begins to get a sense of what solutions are possible within the Stage 1 parameters.

   Mary compares the first car she looks at to the second car. Then she evaluates the features of each additional car she looks at to determine what she likes and doesn't like about each one. So she begins to get a more defined sense of the specific attributes of cars that are available and which features are more important to her. During her search, Mary finds that leather seats feel great, and so leather seats become an important feature in her search for a car.

Now that Mary has defined a specific set of features (leather seats and other things) to look for, she can narrow the comparison to between 3 and 5 actual contenders, and these contenders are now compared. The goal is to eliminate any weaker options and identify the best option through a more rigorous comparison. For example, Mary investigates possible risks and risk mitigation, such as each car's warranty, and any published reviews or safety recalls. By the end of this stage, Mary can rank her options in order of preference, and even begin to feel that a favorite is emerging.

4. **HOW STAGE 2 LEADS TO THE NEXT STAGE**

By the end of Stage 2, the decision maker has clarified what is important in the decision. The decision maker has narrowed her search to a small pool of three to five real options which can be ranked in order of preference. Now one favorite is beginning to emerge. So this decision maker is ready to move into Stage 3, where the focus narrows down to one best choice.

Stage 3: Emergence

1. **STAGE 3, DEFINED**

In Stage 3, Emergence, the decision maker eliminates the remaining alternatives and works her way toward her final choice. This decision maker takes action by making a commitment, permanently giving up the alternatives, and burning the bridges.

2. **STAGE 3, DESCRIBED**

In Stage 3, the decision maker is ready to eliminate the remaining options and narrow down the choices to one favorite choice. This is the steep downhill slope of the decision because, as this decision maker eliminates and narrows her options, then her favorite option starts to gain momentum. Now she works to focus all her attention on the one best option, to hold her focus on this option until she's ready to take action by making a commitment. In making this commitment to the one best option, she permanently gives up the alternatives, and burning the bridges to these alternatives. The commitment part of this stage is represented by a leap across a canyon. I think it's appropriate.

3. **STAGE 3, EXAMPLE**

    I will continue here with the example I offered above, for Stages 1 and 2, applying this Baseline Decision Making Model to Mary and her car purchase. In Stage 3, Mary needs to start building momentum around one emerging choice, in this case one favorite car, so that she can leave the other options behind. She starts to feel that a Subaru is her favorite, so she tests her feeling of preference for the Subaru by going for another test drive. She invites a friend to come look at the Subaru with her, seeking this friend's opinion about the choice. These tests can serve to *add momentum to the choice*.

    As Mary reaches the end of this stage, she fully commits to the Subaru by acting on her decision, giving up her alternatives and burning bridges. She trades in her old car, pays and signs the paperwork for the new car. She negotiates with the dealer to include some custom floor mats which can't be returned. She throws away the other car brochures and information she has collected during her evaluation of her options.

4. **HOW STAGE 3 LEADS TO THE NEXT STAGE**

    By the end of Stage 3, the decision maker has made her decision, given up her alternatives and burned her bridges. Now this decision maker has made it across the canyon. Now this decision maker's Difference Engine starts to behave differently, setting her up to feel good about, even love, her decision in Stage 4.

Stage 4: Reinforcement

1. **STAGE 4, DEFINED**

    Finally, once the decision maker makes it across the canyon, she gets to the best part: Stage 4, Reinforcement. This is where this decision maker begins to really love this decision, to feel quite satisfied with it.

2. **STAGE 4, DESCRIBED**

In Stage 4, the decision maker is fully committed to her decision. Now the decision maker's emotions "own" and invest themselves in the decision. So now these emotions like this decision even better. In this Stage 4, this decision maker invests time in using the benefits of this choice that are most appealing to her. This decision maker may even make efforts to take care of and protect her choice.

The Difference Engine is quite active here in Stage 4. This decision maker's Difference Engine works to further set the choice apart from all the other options, backfilling and supporting this feeling with whatever available data actually concurs with how she feels about this choice. The Difference Engine even looks for new benefits of, and uses for, the choice that has been made. And the Difference Engine may even go ahead and seek social support for this choice from others. In Stage 4, Reinforcement, this decision maker feels a strong sense of inner harmony regarding her choice. Harmony drowns out any doubt or regret, to the point that these fade away.

3. **STAGE 4, EXAMPLE**

Let's continue with Mary's example. In Stage 4, moving through this baseline model in making this decision, Mary's Difference Engine starts to behave differently. At this stage, the Difference Engine no longer notices other cars or provides any comparisons for her. Instead, this Difference Engine starts noticing any information that reinforces and affirms her Subaru. Mary suddenly starts noticing other Subarus on the road when she is out driving. She is now feeling drawn to positive articles or reviews about her car. She will gloss over, ignore, or simply not see any negative information about her new car.

To deepen her emotional investment in her new Subaru, Mary looks for new benefits and uses for her car, and invest more time in using the benefits that are most appealing to her. She takes a drive with the sunroof open, and plans a road trip to the mountains to try out her new car in the snow. She makes efforts to take care of and protect her Subaru, such as washing it and buying a new car vacuum. The act of caring for the car she has chosen is an investment of her time and energy in her choice. And this investment increases her sense of the car's value.

All of these efforts serve to increase Mary's satisfaction and happiness with her new car. And all this serves to affirm her decision so that she feels great about herself as a decision maker.

4. **HOW STAGE 4 BRINGS THIS PROCESS TO CONCLUSION**

Enjoyment of the choice that was made is now enhanced by a sense of self-satisfaction that gives the decision maker more confidence in her ability to make great decisions and thus create a good life for herself. This happiness makes her next decisions flow all the more smoothly, with less ambiguity and doubt.

Individual Decision Processes Vary

Your individual decision process, including how you think through decisions and the way you feel about them, will vary from this baseline model. But the underlying architecture of your thought process in decision making is the same. You do go through the four basic decision stages of the baseline model, although some decision processes compress or abbreviate some stages so much that they are barely detectable.

The important thing to know is that your individual decision process is a great thing. Your individual style is often much better than this baseline model could ever be. However, your decision process might be interacting with your thought processes to create more doubt and ambiguity for you than you'd like. In Part Four, you'll learn about the strengths and weaknesses of your own decision process so that you can take full advantage of what you do best while better understanding and reducing some of the doubt that you might be experiencing.

CHAPTER 10

Decoding Your Soul Type

N ow that you have a Baseline Decision Making Process for comparison, the next step is to see how your decision process is different from that model. In Part Four, you will be able to identify your soul type, and read about the specific decision process that is characteristic of your soul type.

Your soul type tells us how you are creative in the world and how you solve problems. These creative differences between us can be grouped into seven different, distinct soul types. These are the: Optimizing Soul; Learning Soul; Efficient Soul; Coaching Soul; Expressive Soul; Experimenting Soul; and Collaborative Soul.

Each soul type is particularly good at one aspect of problem solving because of how those individuals think about problems. For example, one soul type is best at figuring out a solution, while another is better at figuring out a plan, or getting people aligned, or getting things moving. Each of us is capable of doing any of these things, but most of us are most interested in one of these aspects of the problem. It's the part we gravitate towards, that we might perceive as being most important to our own feeling of success. The aspect of the problem that you most gravitate towards aligns with your soul type. In any problem:

Someone needs to figure out the solution:
> The **Optimizing Soul** *figures out the problem with a creative approach.*
> The **Learning Soul** *figures out the problem with an analytic approach.*

Someone needs to figure out the plan:
> The **Efficient Soul** *figures out how to best utilize resources.*
> The **Coaching Soul** *figures out how to best utilize people.*

Someone needs to get us aligned:
    The **Expressive Soul** engages people in the vision.

Someone needs to get us moving
    The **Experimenting Soul** pushes solutions forward.
    The **Collaborative Soul** pulls people together.

Whenever work gets done, there are times when each of these skills are needed. We can all do each of these things – in fact, you most likely borrow skills from other soul types at different times. But we each have one soul type that is natural to us that makes us exceptionally good at one of these things. We are problem-solving specialists. We each were born with a soul type that makes us very good at solving a particular kind of problem.

Being a specialist is a good thing. Everyone knows that cardiologists get paid more than general practitioners. However, if you are a specialist, it means you won't be as well rounded as a generalist. Developing expertise on one aspect of a problem frequently comes at the expense of some other aspect of the problem. It is in those points of weakness that ambiguity creeps into your decisions.

Each soul type has a characteristic decision process which enables their specific talents and gifts. Your decision process is the set of behaviors that you use to express the talents and gifts of your soul type. Learning about your decision process gives us a window into and a way to understand the strengths and weakness of your approach to problem solving so that we can identify where doubt is affecting you.

To make this section most useful to you, I'll describe the valuable strength that your decision process enables, and I'll show the specific way in which having this strength creates the potential for ambiguity in your decisions. Then I'll provide some strategies and ideas that can help you to reduce the ambiguity in your decision making.

To Get Started, See This Soul Type Chart

To get started, work your way through, from top to bottom, the flow chart on the next page to find which of these soul types best describes you. When you arrive at the bottom of the chart, you will find seven letters (A through G) next to the seven boxes pictured there. These letters correspond to the seven soul types I will further describe in Part Four.

A note here: If you find yourself uncertain how to answer one or more of the questions on this flow chart, don't worry. Choose one or more of the final seven letters that are most likely to fit you. Then, in Part Four, you will be able to read the description for each soul type that might apply to you, and find the one that feels most right to you.

Another important note: It's likely that you will use skills from more than one soul type in your life, and that the skills you apply depends on the type of problem or situation you are facing. People sometimes borrow the skills from another soul type when they're at work, but revert to their natural soul type behavior at home. People sometimes use skills from another soul type for stressful decisions that could affect their personal or financial well being. Even so, we have a natural soul type that fits us best and that we express most of the time.

Read about your own soul type based on the letter you give yourself based on this Soul Type Flow Chart. To find the chapter that fits the letter the chart brought you to, see this list:

The 7 Soul Types

A	The Optimizing Soul	(see Chapter 11)
B	The Learning Soul	(see Chapter 12)
C	The Efficient Soul	(see Chapter 13)
D	The Coaching Soul	(see Chapter 14)
E	The Expressive Soul	(see Chapter 15)
F	The Experimenting Soul	(see Chapter 16)
G	The Collaborative Soul	(see Chapter 17)

Now, flow through the chart to arrive at the soul type that most fit you....

Start at the top of this Soul Type Flow Chart. Follow the arrows as you answer these questions about your decision making process. Your soul type will be the letter you choose at the bottom of this chart.

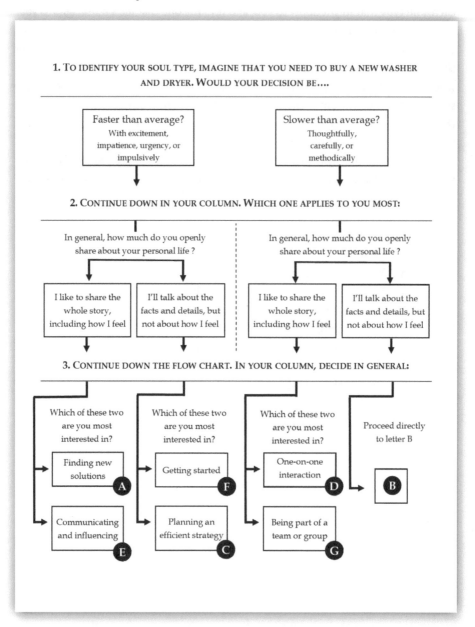

Part Four
Your Soul Type and Decision Process

CHAPTER 11

The Optimizing Soul

Innovative problem solving

Does This Sound Like You?

Are you highly visual? Are you unconventional, and do you gravitate to things that are unusual or unique? Have you or would you like to remodel a house? If you answered yes to at least two of these questions, then you've probably found the right soul type.

What You Are Best At

If you are an Optimizing Soul, your decision process is designed to refine, improve, renovate, renew, and rethink everything - what you have, what you do, and how you do it. This style makes you an incredible problem solver. You have the ability to make things better for people through innovative solutions that combine disparate elements in new, exciting, and unconventional ways. You enjoy solving practical problems, such as streamlining business processes, looking for more efficient ways of doing things, or improving existing spaces and environments.

What Your Decision Process Looks Like

In general, Stage One (Orientation) for you is pretty close to the Baseline Decision Making Process, although it may take longer for you because this is when you do your creative thing. If you are simply choosing between available solutions, you may breeze through this stage quickly. But if you are problem solving, you will need to take the time to see your problem clearly, think it through from different angles, and see if you get inspired with a great idea. Once you have an idea, the rest of your decision process unfolds quickly.

Compared to the baseline decision model, your style is most different in stage 2. In the baseline model, the difference engine is very objective in stage 2. It searches for and compares alternatives, starting with a broad search and narrowing down. The decision maker is relatively impartial and doesn't have any strong feelings of preference about any of the alternatives until they get closer to the end of phase 2, when they can rank the best options in order of preference. In contrast, your stage 2 looks much different. You don't start with an objective, broad search. Instead, you will see something or think of an idea and you will fall in love with it very quickly towards the beginning of stage 2. This changes how you look for data and information.

When you do your research, rather than searching objectively for all the information about your decision, you might just look for information that can quickly confirm if your idea is right. In other words, you search for information that will confirm your choice, and you might pass by or ignore information that disagrees with your choice. The logic is that, if the choice you're considering had a positive outcome before, then it will probably work for you, too. This is actually a very effective short cut which speeds up your decision-making, and it gives you an accurate result most of the time.

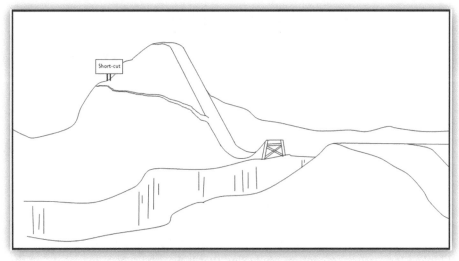

YOUR OPTIMIZING SOUL DECISION PROCESS

*Your decision process has a short cut. This short cut bypasses much of Stage 2
by only searching for information that confirms and supports your idea.*

What's important about this aspect of your decision style is what it allows you to do. The fact that you love your choices early makes it possible for you to bring truly innovative ideas to life. One of the biggest blocks to creativity and innovation is self-doubt. It's very easy to shoot ideas down in phase two. If you paid more attention to the potential risks or reasons your ideas might fail, you might lack the confidence and momentum to carry your ideas through. Your decision style creates enough space for your ideas to grow into something, and provides enough accuracy to still make you a reliably good decision maker, even with this more abbreviated process.

Where Doubt Creeps In

You probably have no trouble falling in love with your decisions most of the time – you are very future focused and, in your mind, you are already imagining being there on the other side of the canyon enjoying your new decision. For you, making the big leap of commitment almost seems like an afterthought.

When You are Choosing between/among Available Solutions

The aspect of your decision style that can sometimes get you into trouble is exactly this: you are ready to leap too quickly. This is where doubt can get you. Sure, the short cut you take in Stage 2, searching only for information that confirms your choice is good, works great most of the time. It's very efficient, and you'll get a great result often enough to keep doing this. However, the risk of quickly falling in love with a choice is that later you may realize that there was some critical piece of information you missed that has in the end made your choice really disappointing. (Here you may experience the *cognitive dissonance* I refer to below.*)

When I went to tour my undergraduate college, I had already decided that I really wanted to like it because of its fantastic international study program. At the time, 60% of each of its graduating classes spent at least one semester overseas, and they had study programs in countries no other school went to. As I walked around the campus, I looked for reasons to confirm my feeling that it was the school for me. I saw the beautiful campus and the small class sizes.

Somehow, I didn't pay any attention to the clear evidence of the school culture, which had time-warped back to the late 1960's. Looking back now, I can't imagine how I missed it, except for the fact that I know I was deliberately seeking confirming information, and we only see what we are looking for. Once I arrived as a new student, the culture felt oddly conformist and confining, and it wasn't a great fit for me. Unwilling to wear Birkenstocks, play bongo drums, or make dream pillows, I had to then make sense of my decision and undergraduate experience as a character-building exercise.

One strategy for avoiding this problem in your decision making is to, once you have a solution in mind, try to prove yourself wrong. You will most likely hate doing this. However, this is one of the absolute best techniques for fast and accurate decision making. If you are writing the important points from this book to put on sticky-notes above your desk, this should be one of them: *try to prove yourself wrong to know if you are right.*

Notes on Reducing Your Doubt

If your family was ever prone to driving long distances on vacation, you have probably played the game 20 Questions (this is a much better car game than "Slug Bug," which I always found painful.) To play the game, one person thinks of something that can be classified as an animal, a mineral, or a vegetable. The other players have up to 20 yes-or-no questions to guess what the item is.

How you ask your questions has a great deal to do with whether you win or lose. Let's say that the item we are guessing has been classified as an animal. You may start by asking if it has four legs and fur. Does it eat plants? Is it wild? Does it live in North America? Is it bigger than a bicycle? As you get more yes answers to your questions, you will begin to develop a hypothesis. In this case, it sounds a lot like a deer. Sadly, this is wrong. Let's back up and try that differently.

Looking for Disconfirming Information

Does it eat plants? Yes. Does it eat things other than plants? Yes! Is it wild? Yes. Is it ever not wild? Yes! Now we are looking for something quite different. There aren't too many domesticated omnivores, so we have narrowed the field dramatically – mostly to pigs. We did this by looking for *disconfirming information*, and it's one of the quickest ways to get a correct answer when you're making decisions.

Searching for negative information about your choice helps you to find the gaps in your thinking much more rapidly, and thus can improve the momentum of your decision. This search helps you to avoid *cognitive dissonance** later and gives you more faith in your ability to make good decisions. You will still like the choice you make just as much – once you commit to it. And, any faults you find in your decision process *become known contours in your landscape and therefore fade into the background*. When I was choosing my school, if I had been aware of the culture and decided to go there anyway, my feeling about my choice to go there would have been different. I would have accepted it more easily and enjoyed the reasons I went there more thoroughly. This is because I would have made my choice while allowing myself to see the *disconfirming information* while I made the choice.

When You are Inventing New Solutions

Some of your decision making is going to involve developing new solutions to problems as opposed to choosing between available, already in existence, solutions. In this case, you will spend extra time in Stage 1, thinking through the problem in new ways to come up with a great new idea. Sometimes Stage 1 can take you a little longer than others would expect because of how you think. Your own thought process may not be linear like most peoples'. "A" doesn't always take you directly to "B," and then directly to "C" like it would if you were doing things in the expected way. Part of how you are creative is by starting with "A" and then jumping to "N", and then over to the number "3." You combine things in new ways and use things unconventionally. You might think of a way to apply a manufacturing process to a software quality test organization. You might use a tree branch for a shower curtain rod. If you try to explain this to other people who don't know where you're headed, this might make no sense to them at all.

Once you have a great idea, your vision and end state may be clear in your mind. However, the path to get there may take more time to fully develop since you aren't following an established route. It's not always clear how all the pieces will fit together. The problem you can run into is that you may be focused on your future vision and ignoring gaps or obstacles that will become more apparent as your ideas are expressed. This is where your Stage 2 short-cut comes in. You are thinking ahead and imagining your idea in action, searching only for confirming information that pushes your idea forward, and not focusing on the details or problems standing in your way.

You may want to develop the habit of taking time to think through a linear progression of what you are proposing, to examine what assumptions you are making and how each step will occur. You would benefit from thinking through what the obstacles might be at each stage of your idea, and what the possible risks could be. Not only will this process help uncover any gaps, but it will also help to make concepts more concrete.

- To help speed up the process of defining your ideas, set aside time in your day where you can think things through and problem solve. Any time you can find where you can be quiet but engaged in a habitual physical activity such as walking, folding laundry, or brushing your teeth, something that leaves your mind free to think, will help you to process and connect your thoughts and ideas.
- Involve other people in your thinking process. Bring in people who are more data driven and who will see and point out the gaps in your thinking. Fair warning – this will be frustrating for both you and the people you bring in – but in the end, you will get where you want to go much faster and with better results.

- After you decide, stop shopping. Once you have made your choice, resist the temptation to double-check your choice. At this point, you should be finished with information gathering and comparison.

Confirmation Shopping

Because you move so quickly through phase two, you might be mid-leap, half way across the canyon, when you experience twinges of doubt creeping in. Somewhere in the back of your mind is the awareness that you didn't really do your due diligence. When you feel this, you might try to cope with your doubt by double-checking to see if you made the right choice. This is called confirmation shopping. The idea is to look at a few alternatives you hadn't bothered to consider before just to prove to yourself that you picked the best one.

I used to be super guilty of confirmation shopping. I made an offer on a house once, and while I waited for the seller's response, I asked my agent if she would to take me to see a few other houses, just to be sure I had chosen the right one. Not only was this a waste of my time and hers, but it didn't settle anything. It just made me feel uneasy.

I've done the same thing with all kinds of purchases. Many times, before I took the tags off my purchase, I would go out and check the price of the same item elsewhere. I went to other stores to see if I had gotten a good deal. Once I bought a pair of nice black pants but was uneasy about my purchase, so a few days later I stopped by a different store just to confirm that my pants were better than what this other store had. However, once I saw the pants at this other store, I wasn't sure, so I bought those, too. Now I had two pair of pants and was dissatisfied with both.

If you have ever played fetch with a Labrador and thrown two tennis balls for him at the same time, you have seen the dog try and hold two balls in its mouth at once. I am equally unable to wear both pair of pants at once. I have never felt better after confirmation shopping – I have always felt worse.

We may start confirmation shopping with good intentions, but the process generally makes us feel badly. Confirmation shopping introduces doubt back into your decision. Instead of looking for what is good about the decision you made, your *difference engine* reverts to Stage 2 and starts comparing your choice against the new alternative. You are hoping in good faith that the choice you have already made will be better, but there is some chance that it won't. In some cases, confirmation shopping will push you all the way back to Stage 1 and you will have to start the entire decision over again.

Stop Shopping

If you have gone through the pre-decision process before making your commitment, then you are as sure as you are going to be. Continuing to look for new options to compare against is back-tracking in the process and, instead of giving you the confidence you are looking for, it will actually make you feel much worse. Stop shopping and focus on what you like about the choice you made.

CHAPTER 12

The Learning Soul

Analytic problem solving

Does This Sound Like You?

Do you develop deep knowledge about the subjects that interest you? Are you pragmatic and practical? Do you have or have you considered getting an advanced degree? If you answered yes to at least two of these questions, then you've probably found the right soul type.

What You Are Best At

If you use the Learning Style of decision making, you use rigor, logic, and analysis to improve the quality of your decisions. This approach is highly analytic. It enables you to remain open minded, objective, and pragmatic much longer than any other decision style and to use information and analysis to understand all parts of an issue.

As someone who applies this learning style to your decision making, you have the ability to develop a deep knowledge and understanding of the subject areas that you find relevant to your decision process. And you will seek out all available input and information about a topic before coming to a conclusion. You have a talent for figuring things out and your expertise and analytic mind make you an excellent problem solver.

What Your Decision Process Looks Like

When your decision process unfolds smoothly, it can look somewhat like the Baseline Decision Making Process, however your process has a slightly expanded Stage 1 and Stage 2. You don't like to be rushed. Your excellent analytical skills have always served you well, and you need a certain amount of time to put them to use in your decision process.

When you can, you would rather take a scenic, methodical route, leaving enough time for research, discovery, learning and reflection. With your careful, analytical method, you can be more certain to get a good result and you get to learn some interesting things along the way.

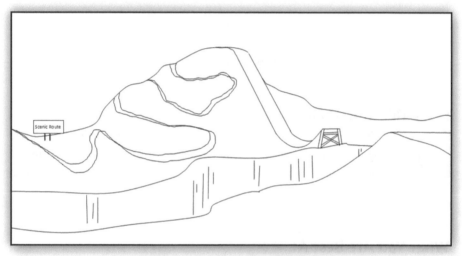

Scenic Route

YOUR LEARNING DECISION PROCESS
Your Learning decision process remains objective.
Your style has a slow, thoughtful, analytic slope to the decision point.

The key aspect of your decision process is your ability to approach most decisions with detached objectivity. When it comes to your decisions, you are a lot more like Star Trek's Spock than Captain Kirk because you are able to stay in a neutral, logical frame of mind and keep your emotions out of a decision longer than other people can. This means you can be more open minded, and you will give fair consideration to ideas that other people might reject too quickly.

While your learning soul type is very open to new ideas and information, you have a cautious decision process that emphasizes methodical analysis. Because of your focus on learning and intellectual exploration, your decisions are made independently; and, you probably prefer information and research that you find for yourself rather than listening to opinions or conclusions from others. You will most likely take a cautious but pragmatic and utilitarian approach to your decisions. You will thus be open to at least considering *whatever* might work and can be applied to the problem at hand.

The benefits of this decision style can become very apparent to you when you are working with others. You see where others have flaws in their logic, or have dismissed important data, or have jumped to incorrect conclusions. You analyze other people's solutions and find their weak spots. You will have the data to confirm or contradict others' conclusions. Your decision style enables the best thinking.

Where Doubt Creeps In

You tend to make good decisions. You have the most data based decision style and you stay open minded longer than anyone else, so you really think things through carefully before you choose. You are pragmatic and logical, so when the best option becomes clear, you have no problem spotting it and moving forward. The problem you may run into is that when you are doubtful or blocked in some way you may stop, observe, and wait for something to change. You wait instead of taking an active role to change the landscape and cut your own path forward or working around the obstacle with a compromise of some sort.

Doubt may be less painful for you than it is for other soul types because you are very comfortable staying in neutral and not deciding. You might like to remain detached and be more of an observer of the problems you are trying to solve. You wait in neutral to see if something in the landscape will change by itself to present a way forward. In general, this means your decisions can stall out and get stuck, so you are going to place fewer bets, and you may miss out on opportunities.

Ambiguity is a natural output of your wait-and-see approach. You tend to leave things not just unresolved but hanging in mid-air, waiting for a response. This approach to doubt is perfectly comfortable for you, but it may be hard on others. If you delay decisions at work because you are observing the problem, this usually means that your team or organization is left waiting for instructions. Teams and organizations are like big ships in motion. You have to tell them where to go or they will idle, burning fuel and resources, or they will drift without you in a direction you never intended.

Notes on Reducing Your Doubt

The key to balancing out your decision style is to *focus on your momentum*. If you feel a decision stalling out in neutral, keeping some movement forward going, even if it is small, will help you find your path forward sooner. This way you will miss out on fewer opportunities and create less doubt ambiguity for those around you. You can do this by breaking down the problem, by looking for compromises, and by working toward 75% certainty.

Breaking Down the Problem

When my children lose things, I see it as an opportunity to get them to clean their rooms. (The way I see it, there is no harm in killing two birds with one stone.) Under normal circumstances, the chaos of their rooms can be overwhelming and, if I ask them to clean up, they won't know where to start. When they are looking for something, they aren't focusing on the big picture - they are just picking things up one at a time and putting them away. Breaking the mess down into its parts and deciding where to put each separate thing gets them unstuck, brings order to the chaos, and uncovers the thing they were looking for.

Most decisions have many moving parts. If your decision is blocked in some way, there are usually smaller parts of the decision that you can still work on. Even though these smaller things may seem tangential and irrelevant compared to the big obstacle, *moving in small ways works to change the overall landscape*. Each small action you take creates room for change, and as your landscape shifts, a new path forward may be uncovered.

If your obstacle is a conceptual block, where it isn't clear which strategy or direction to take, you can still make progress. There are always small details and practical aspects to any problem, and if you make choices on those small questions, you are reducing your total amount of doubt and ambiguity about the problem as a whole. The small answers begin to guide the larger answer. If you are planning a home remodel and you are waiting to decide on a master plan before you get moving, just chose your tile. Making that one choice will set parameters such as color and style that will guide your next choice. By taking one small step after another, you will start to build the momentum you need to get your decision on track.

Looking for Compromises

When your decision is stalled in doubt, you can often get a better result by finding a path around whatever is blocking you rather than waiting for an optimal solution. A compromise may not seem worthwhile at first, but the factor you aren't including in your analysis is the cost of not moving. This cost of not moving is much higher than you think.

It's easy to only place value on things that we do, action that we do take, and to ignore the consequences of not doing something. People are more troubled when they do something that causes one person to get hit by a bus than they are when their *not* doing something results in 20 people getting hit by a bus. When you are the one driving, you feel you are causing things to happen, so you feel like you are more culpable. If you're standing by and watching, it's easy to stay detached and uninvolved.

The truth is that you aren't independent of your environment – you are part of it, and if your actions could have saved those 20 bus victims, then the fact that you could have saved them but decided not to makes you culpable. You decided not to act, and that carries as much weight as deciding to take action. Both are decisions you make, and both carry responsibility for their outcomes. In fact, many countries, including Finland, Germany, and Israel have rescue or Good Samaritan laws that carry criminal penalties for not acting to save others.

When you don't act, what are you losing? What are the risks of inaction? How pressing is the problem you are trying to solve and what are its risks and impacts? What is the cost of the opportunity you may be missing out on?

Think through any possible compromises that might be riskier or sub-optimal solutions. Weigh their disadvantages against the risks you are taking by not acting. When seen through this more balanced perspective, a compromise that is 75% as good may be significantly better than waiting for a 100% solution.

75% Certainty is Great

When you are in the process of making a decision, the goal is to work your process until you are pretty sure of your choice. If you continue to put in a lot of effort after that point, after you are pretty sure, then you start to get diminishing returns. The importance of those last unresolved details seems to get blown out of proportion. And, the more you grow absorbed in last little details, the harder it will be for you to discern whether they are important. You may over-weight factors that have relatively little impact on your problem, become paralyzed worrying about logical but unlikely contingencies, or obsess about minor details.

The sweet spot is at around 75% certainty. When you are 75% sure that your solution will work and your doubts and worries are limited to 25%, you can have confidence that you are making a good decision and you are moving fast enough to build momentum.

THE SLOPE TO 75%
The slope to 75% certainty is productive, however after that, the last 25% diminishes in value.

The remaining 25% of uncertainty is really hard to resolve. Often there is no clear answer and it slows you down to a crawl, which creates the opportunity for you to notice more things that you can worry about.

If you focus on the remaining 25% that you are unsure about, you over work it. Then the best solution starts to blend in with all the others. And the benefits of all the different options start to stick together. With no outstanding option that you can fix on, you start to spin in place, stuck in doubt, and your satisfaction with whatever choice you eventually make goes way down.

Go for It

Understand that *the momentum of your decision process* is as important to your success as is the decision itself. When you get stuck focusing on that last 25% of unresolved detail, you are sabotaging your decision. In decision making there are usually many different paths that could all work to some degree – there is no one true best way. So success is defined by how you feel about your choice. Your choice will feel successful if you feel great about it. If you get stuck in the last 25%, you are almost certain not to feel great about your decision and you will thus have regrets and doubt. This means that your decision will not feel successful no matter what that decision is.

So when you find a solution that is 75% great, let go. Have faith that things will turn out for the best, and go for it.

CHAPTER 13

The Efficient Soul

Figuring out how to best utilize resources

Does This Sound Like You?

s work your primary hobby? Are you comfortable being assertive and taking charge? Are you usually able to take standardized tests quickly? If you answered yes to at least two of these questions, then you've probably found the right soul type.

What You Are Best At

With the Efficient Style of decision making, you strategize the best use of your resources and abilities for the fastest and most efficient path to long-range success. You are able to identify and attack the fewest critical actions that need to be done for the most efficient path forward.

What Your Decision Process Looks Like

This is a big picture, bottom line approach. Your decision process is so methodical and efficient that it may look like the Baseline Decision Making Process. However, you will move through each of the basic Baseline Decision Making Process stages with fast and effective precision. You don't like to wait, and will push for action at every step. Through the whole process, you'll be looking for and re-evaluating the fastest possible route forward with the best use of resources. Where needed, you will be adapting your decision process quickly, in real time.

You make decisions in the same way that you might play chess. When you analyze a problem or objective, you reduce all the elements down to their strategic values. Then you evaluate the broader view of the overall goal or problem to determine the best placement for each of the resources, the *strategic distribution* that will enable the best performance. There is a level of detachment in your analysis which enables you to see all the pieces of the game for their value to your mission without the distraction of sentimental, emotional, or nostalgic ties. You will know when you need to sacrifice a pawn in order to save your queen, or sacrifice your queen to win the game.

Because your decision process is so efficient, you tend to make decisions yourself, pretty much on your own. You do this independently, although you may involve others in brainstorming to suggest useful, goal oriented ideas and solutions. You know making decisions quickly and relatively independently carries some risk, but your Efficient soul type is comfortable embracing and managing risk.

The strategic nature of your decision style, along with your ability to distill complex elements down to what is most relevant and important to your decision, enables you to be a fantastic chess player, both on a chess board and in life. You thrive in a position where you have strategic control over whatever context you are in.

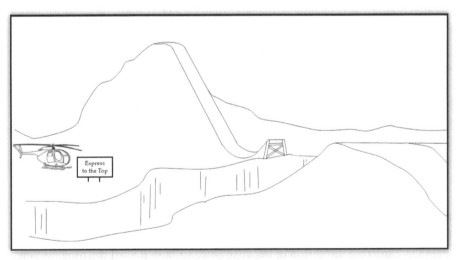

YOUR EFFICIENT DECISION PROCESS
Your Efficient decision process identifies the fastest and most effective strategy.
You choose the path that allows you to move forward most quickly and effectively.

Where That Doubt Creeps in

Your Efficient style may be pretty close to the Baseline Decision Making Process. Your style is fast, efficient, and thorough. You know how to spend just enough time in each stage and you don't take any obvious short cuts. Where you run into problems is when your decisions involve or affect other people. You could be halfway to your destination before you look behind you and realize that no one has come along. Even if you feel pretty satisfied with your choices, the people who work with you and for you will be stuck in Stage 1 with no chance of moving forward. You are a natural leader, but in order to fulfill that potential, you need to help your team come with you.

Your decision process is quite self-reliant. You really do find it more efficient to make your decisions independently. You may not be accustomed to asking other people for ideas and input, or even sharing your own thinking about a decision. You may be decisive and confident enough to inspire others to follow you (whether or not they have contributed anything to your decision process). But they won't know where they are going and so won't be able to fully bring their own skills and talents to your effort.

A few years ago, I facilitated a planning meeting for a very successful executive who I will call CEO Mr. Henry. His goal for the meeting was to have his team discuss and share ideas about his business strategy. But he was concerned that if he stayed in the room, the members of the team would hold back and let him speak for them. He decided that at the beginning of the discussion he would leave the room to "take a call" so that his team would have the chance to discuss his strategy among themselves.

So CEO Henry left the room, with me in charge. I stood there, next to a blank flip chart, my pen in hand, prompting them with questions and waiting for someone to respond. They all just looked awkwardly at each other. No one had any idea what to say. These were not inexperienced people – they were all very accomplished executives in a large Fortune 500 organization. None of them could define their boss's business strategy, and they had no idea where he was headed with his decision. When their boss came back into the room, it was the first moment he realized that his team was completely in the dark and had no idea what he was thinking.

In his own mind, his strategy was crystal clear, but because he hadn't included his team in his decision process they were totally unaware of his thinking. When this happens you might as well put your business in neutral and let the engine idle. Team members can't take ownership of the goals or contribute toward the progress when they don't know where you are going and why.

Not only will being in the dark make people less effective, but it will also make them unsatisfied. It isn't enough for them to trust that you've made the best choice.

If they don't go through the process of comparing alternatives and emotionally committing to your path, they will have too much ambiguity and doubt about what they are doing to feel good about it. They have to buy in and commit to your plan, and they can't do that if they don't have the information they need to participate.

Notes on Reducing Your Doubt

To reduce the ambiguity being experienced by the people you work with, you may want to make a deliberate effort to include others more effectively in your decision process. Some ways to do this are to get input, to over communicate, and to decentralize the decision making.

Get Input

Make room for other people's ideas. You may have a tendency to take over conversations (because you probably already have a good answer) so you will need to resist that impulse and let others find their way to a solution. Deliberately ask for input and then give people time to think and respond. Other people need time to process their thoughts, so be prepared to give them a reasonable time frame in which to get back to you. Remember that asking for input isn't just about getting the best answer. It also accomplishes something you need, which is other people's engagement.

One way to involve stakeholders in your, now also their, decision process is to brainstorm issues and questions such as perceived risks, possible problems and concerns. Share your ideas with them, get their comments and suggestions about your ideas. Then also share accountability with them, such as allowing them to participate in investigating the results, and committing to report any conclusions. This will involve stakeholders in the decision process so that they have the opportunity to understand the decision rationale. This can help dispel any concerns they may have and can allow them to more fully support the execution of this decision.

Over Communicate

Your thought process is very internal so you are in no danger of saying too much. Aim to communicate twice as much about your ideas as you think is necessary, and you will probably be right on target.

You might prefer to be more directive in your communication style because it is a fast and efficient way for you to get things done. But this doesn't always lead to other people helping you most effectively. When you talk about your ideas and plans, in addition to communicating what you want to do, be sure to also communicate why. Explain your rationale and what is influencing your conclusions so that other people understand your thinking. Tell the story of your idea and how it evolved, why it's important, and what it will create.

Decentralize Decision Making

Because of your independent and efficient decision making style, you may operate in a command and control fashion, where all the information comes into you and all the decisions come out. This can work well to get things done, *but this isn't very scalable,* meaning that it gets harder and harder to operate this way as your responsibilities and the scale of your problems grow. This is a common issue for leaders of large organizations. They may overlook the scale of their decision processes, and find themselves handling all levels of everything the same way.

I once watched the CEO of a very big company get involved in the decision regarding whether or not to keep a few hard drives from some old computers that were being recycled. At a certain point, you just don't have time to work that way. Chances are that you'll feel overworked because you take on responsibility for all aspects of your business or your life. If you are being involved in decision making at every level of your organization, or in all important aspects of your home life, you are taking too much control.

Learning to share decision making responsibility or to decentralize it and push responsibility for decisions out to other family members, or down into your organization, will accomplish several important things. It will make you less busy and more able to focus on things that are important to you. This sharing of decision making responsibility reduces ambiguity for the people around you because it allows them to take ownership of some aspect of the work. They are more involved in and have a better understanding of your planning and decision making.

CHAPTER 14

The Coaching Soul

Figuring out how to best utilize people

Does This Sound Like You?

Does your work involve directly serving the health, wellbeing, needs, or development of others? Is your life centered on your family and friends? Are you good at organizing and developing processes to manage work that you are responsible for? If you answered yes to at least two of these questions, then you've probably found the right soul type.

What You Are Best At

The Coaching soul type is able to bring out the best in others by enabling their growth and development and inspiring their best contributions. You are able to see past the self-limitations that hold people back and focus in on what is best about them. For you, those qualities that you admire in someone become who they are to you. Because you see them that way, you hold the space for them to become their best selves.

When people look at you, you reflect back to them that best version of themselves. Through your eyes, they see themselves as they want to be, and it inspires them to live up to that vision. These qualities make you an amazing healer, manager and developer of people.

You are focused on individual connections with people, connections you make that are driven by altruism and empathy for others. You foster an environment that prioritizes people.

What Your Decision Process Looks Like

When your decisions proceed smoothly, your Coaching decision making process includes all four of the Baseline Decision Making Process stages. But compared to the Baseline, you will spend more time in Stages 1 and 2.

This is because you are cautious and protective in your approach. You are probably not the type to go out looking for change, but if change is necessary, you will tend to be practical and pragmatic, and you will find a relatively conservative, moderate path that prioritizes safety.

An important aspect of your decision style is your focus on the well being of others. There is an element of service that you bring to decision making which is noble and inspiring. You tend to prioritize the needs of others above your own. In your desire to care for others you can be protective and hesitant as you evaluate the need for change and the degree of change that is necessary.

YOUR COACHING DECISION PROCESS
Your Coaching soul type is conservative,
careful, cautious, protective, and empathetic

Your cautious style enables you to be responsive and supportive of people. Change can be difficult and painful, so your reluctance to change reflects your understanding of the importance of quality of life and your care for others who might be impacted or upset by an issue or a decision.

Where Doubt Creeps In

In simple decisions, you may breeze through your process and easily settle on a choice you like. However, in more complicated or complex decisions, you might have more trouble. The same ability that enables you to see the best in people also allows you to see and appreciate what is best about each of your decision options. You might find that, in some of your decisions, you have a hard time choosing between things.

Considering and comparing all the various benefits your options can slow you down, and your decision making might take too long, which can impact your momentum and create room for doubt. When the process of choosing stretches on too long or stalls out, your Difference Engine doesn't slow down or stop and wait for you. It's like a motor that stays on and keeps idling, doing its job of comparing even if you aren't moving.

If you have ever made muffins from a box, from one of those muffin mixes, you probably read the directions that instructed you not to over mix the batter. If you made those muffins before you had your coffee, you might not have seen that part of the instructions. Ideally, you want your muffins to be light and fluffy, but when you over-mix the batter, you flatten all the air out of your dough, so your muffins become tough and chewy. This is how you make really bad muffins. In the same way, if you spend too much time over working a decision, the advantages and disadvantages start to stick together and facts become tough and unworkable.

You can over work decisions the way you can overwork batter. When you are in this situation, the first time your Difference Engine shows you something good about an alternative, your emotions will have a vivid response. If time goes by and you still haven't made a commitment, the Difference Engine will keep working to find benefits and differences, and it will start to show you some of the same ones over again. Each subsequent time you revisit a benefit, its value starts to fade in your mind. It's like hearing a joke a second time. It's no longer fresh.

Since you're not making any headway, your difference engine will work even harder and will start to show you some of the benefits of the alternatives you rejected. These will become more vivid in your mind than they were before. The difference between your alternatives starts to shrink, and making a choice gets harder than ever. It becomes chewy and tough, like over-worked dough. Making it out of that sludge is hard work, and if you manage to eventually get to a decision, the sad thing is that you will be less happy with your final choice - even if it was the best one that you could make.

Notes on Reducing Your Doubt

When you are making decisions, there are ways you can help yourself keep your momentum and increase your satisfaction with your decision. There are some steps you can take such as: to decide where to compromise, to clarify your variables, and to limit your options.

Decide Where to Compromise

To increase the momentum of your decision process, try to decide up front what is most important to you and – even more importantly – what you will compromise on. When defining the variables at play in your decision, something's got to give. In any choice you make, there are three elements, like three points of a triangle: *time, quality, and cost*. If you pull on any one of these three points, the other two are affected. If you need more time, be prepared to pay more or sacrifice quality. If quality is most important, then cost and time go up.

My daughter decided to test this theory by refusing to be born. As we went weeks past her due date, I knew she was getting really squished in there because I am not a very tall person, but she had absolutely no interest in coming out. We finally had to induce labor, and my doctor came in to check on us thirty minutes into the Pitocin. My doctor paused and got that calm, serious bedside manner voice. At that moment, I knew that one of the points on the triangle had suddenly constricted. We had no time. My daughter was stressed and not getting enough oxygen, so we had to get her out immediately. Instantly, the room was swarming with people in baggy green uniforms. They wheeled us into a surgery room filled with tons of equipment and even more green people, plus a few more doctors. Twenty minutes later, my daughter was safely out and all was well. There were two points on that triangle that couldn't budge – time and quality. That meant that money had to be spent, so the hospital threw all of its re-sources, equipment, and people at the problem, regardless of expense. Yay, insurance.

If you are in charge of finding larger office space for your growing company and you want to save a lot of money, you are going to have to spend more time hunting for a great deal or give up some quality and move to a less desirable building. If you are buying a new pair of shoes and quality is most important to you, be prepared to spend more money or to spend time waiting for the shoes you want to go on sale. Be clear with yourself about which of the three points are most important to you and on which one you are willing to compromise. Don't waste your time and energy looking for the magic option that will give you all three. This will just lead to frustration and loss of momentum.

Clarify Your Variables

I like to build and renovate houses. Call it a hobby. Over the years, I've become a pro at selecting great tradespeople to work on my various projects. When I meet tradespeople, I look for two things that I've determined are the most important factors for me. First, I get a sense for their expertise. Second, I want to know if they are yes persons or no persons.

To find out, I start by pointing out some questionable aspect of my project, such as I want to move this thing that shouldn't be moved. A no person will tell me how hard it is to do what I am asking, shake his head, make a few disgruntled noises, and generally set my expectation that his bill will be large. A yes person, on the other hand, will grab his coveralls out of his truck and climb up into my spider filled attic to check and see how it might be possible to do what I am asking.

I only hire yes people. Knowing what I'm looking for helps me focus on what is important to me, and helps me tune out distractions. I may meet a contractor who wears booties every time he comes in the door, offers a twelve month guarantee, and gives me wholesale pricing on my materials. But if he's a no person, none of that will matter. It makes choosing the tradesperson I want to work with much easier.

Clearly defining and prioritizing your variables helps you to build momentum in your decision making process. This is because you have thought through what is most important to you. Now your comparison of the alternatives can be focused and efficient.

Limit Yourself to Four or Five Options

Americans are gluttonous about choice. Entire ice cream empires are built on the idea of more choices than you could ever hope to try and still fit in your pants. We associate choice with freedom, and so it becomes something fundamental to being American. The problem is that having too many choices gets in the way of making a decision.

There is a wonderful plant nursery near my home called Flower World. Flower World is so big that you have to use a map to find your way around. It has entire buildings dedicated just to roses, or evergreen shrubs, or grasses. It's a beautiful, multi-acre property complete with giant fountains, wandering chickens, and a petting zoo. I can spend hours at Flower World, but I hate to admit that I rarely buy anything. It's not that I don't need plants – I go fully intending to find the perfect thing and buy it.

The problem is that there are so many perfect things that I get overwhelmed. In the end it's much easier just to leave empty handed. I find that, if I really want to buy plants, I'm better off finding a Flower Village as opposed to a Flower World. If I have to evaluate dozens of choices, my Difference Engine gets tired. It's really hard to keep track of the differences between thirty varieties of fuchsias. If I limit my choices to just four or five, it becomes much easier to evaluate them.

In the event you muster your endurance, spend several hours at Flower World, and are able to come to a final decision about the fuchsias, your reward for all that work will likely be short changed. Instead of loving your choice, you'll end up feeling worse about it. Having lots and lots of options raises your expectations.[v] You begin to expect perfection. Even though you may buy the best fuchsia plant you've ever bought, you end up feeling worse about it. Since you had so many options, if the one you chose isn't perfect, you assume that you picked the wrong one and blame yourself for your dissatisfaction.

In this way, too many alternatives is a recipe for doubt. Too much choice either puts your Difference Engine to sleep or puts it into hyper-drive and gets it stuck in Stage 2. Now your Difference Engine starts working against you instead of working for you. Limit the number of alternatives you are considering to four or five at the most. Choosing is so much easier when you limit your options. And when you do limit these options to choose from, you are six times more likely to make a decision. In the end you will be a lot happier with your choice.

CHAPTER 15

The Expressive Soul

Engaging people in the vision

Does This Sound Like You?

Are you at home on stage or in front of others? Do you have a natural talent for expressing yourself with words, story, drama or metaphor? Do you hate to lose? If you answered yes to at least two of these questions, then you've probably found the right soul type.

What You Are Best At

The Expressive Style of decision making is influential and persuasive. You are able to create a story, narrative, or metaphor that helps others make emotional sense of their sacrifice, courage, and hard work, and you can connect all this to shared values. You bring a strong instinct for the drama, humor, and emotion that can connect people to their work and give them a sense of shared purpose. Your focus is on communication, alignment, and creating meaning.

What Your Decision Process Looks Like

Your decisions are usually in service to an idea, ideal, or objective that resonates emotionally for you. Your idealism makes decisions that matter to you, not just as an objective exercise, but as a campaign to be won. It follows naturally that you really hate to lose. Your emotional connection makes decision making very personal and subjective for you.

You are strongly connected to your emotions, which means that, compared to the Baseline Decision Making Process, your decision making style can be very fast, glossing over Stages 1 and 2, and moving relatively quickly though the rest of the stages. You may make decisions on impulse.

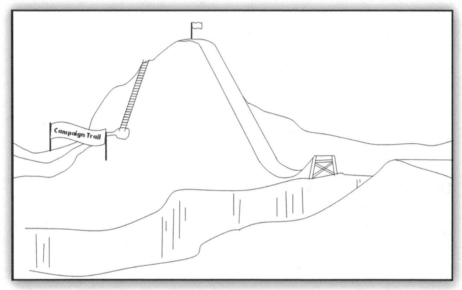

YOUR EXPRESSIVE STYLE

Your Expressive Style is fast moving, persuasive, influential, emotional, impulsive and driven by a sense of purpose or mission.

Impulsiveness in decision-making has a bad rap. We have burdened it by lumping it together with all types of impulsive behavior – everything from kids blurting out in class to adult addiction problems. The common wisdom is that only cautious, methodical decision-making is pro-social and effective. So not true.

Like all decision processes, impulsiveness comes with its own set of strengths and weaknesses. As an Expressive soul type, you are is closely connected to your emotions, and the benefit of using your emotions to make decisions is speed. With this decision process, you can be more persuasive, assertive and influential because, while everyone else is still trying to figure out what they think, you already have a strong point of view. Throw you into any corporate viper-pit and you will be ready at a moment's notice to defend or advocate for what you feel is right. You're faster on your feet than anyone else, and since you're arguing from your emotions, you instinctively know how to find the passion, drama and strength in your argument.

In addition to being fast, persuasive and passionate, you are frequently right. As long as your emotions are informed by an accurate picture of the challenges and goals you are facing, you can fix on the best path forward and drive towards it. You are able to filter out the distractions that might cloud the picture for more plodding decision-makers. You are never tempted to stray from your ideals and values since no amount of cold logic will sway you from what you feel is right.

There is an aspect of bravery in your decision-making because you bring a strong sense of personal honor and loyalty that makes you unafraid to stand up for what feels right. How you feel about each part of a decision is what is most important – your emotions are the compass that guides you.

Where Doubt Creeps In

Given that one of the biggest challenges in creating something is building momentum, your ability to create persuasive urgency and move rapidly is invaluable. Where you might run into problems is in the regulation of your speed. You are like a sports car that has only two settings – super-fast and parked. Rather than working in a steady forward direction, you tend to go impulse-on, impulse-off, like a toggle switch.

You are ruled by your emotions, and they respond with immediacy and to immediacy – to the things that are present right now. Your emotions don't pay as much attention to things that are in the future. So it may be too easy for you to make decisions that feel great in the moment but that you end up regretting down the road. You could end up committing to things that you aren't prepared to follow through on. Similarly, you may say or do things that have longer term consequences you aren't considering, and that aren't great. You could end up with more doubt and buyer's remorse than you would want.

When your toggle-switch is on, there's an urgency to your decisions that pushes you to skip ahead and commit. When the toggle switches to off, you lose interest. Your challenge is to develop something in the middle between the two extremes that allows you the time to build *sustainable momentum* behind a decision so that you can work your way through the four basic Decision Stages and feel satisfied with your choices.

Notes on Reducing Your Doubt

Some strategies that may work for you are to: stay in the game, build layers of resistance, feed your brain, be vigilant about data and information, rank the problem, and set aside the resources you'll need.

Stay in the Game

I enjoy playing tennis, but I'm not a great player. I don't have any spectacular moves, drop shots, killer serves, or well placed lobs in my bag of tricks. If I ever try for the trick shot, that's when I choke. Over time I've come to accept this, and now see it as a strength instead of a weakness. I've learned that if I just focus on returning the ball and getting it over the net, I win more than I lose. My game is about outlasting my competitor. The consistent application of even effort works better than the occasional brilliance of spectacular sprints. As a tennis player, I'm definitely the tortoise, not the hare.

My dad is the master of consistent, even effort. When he was in college, he sold cookware door to door for extra money. By keeping track of how many doors he knocked on each day and how many sales he made, he figured out the ratio of no's to yes's. He came to see his job as collecting no's. He knew exactly how many no's he had to collect before he got to his yes and made a sale. He just had to consistently hit the ball back over the net, and eventually he'd win. He applied the same logic to his studies. He figured out how many hours of studying he had to do for each class in order to get an A. He would keep track of each hour he studied with hash marks on the inner cover of his text book. It became a simple equation of steady, consistent effort to earn the A. He always knew how many hours he had left to put in.

Commit to the Decision

When you commit to a decision, there can be many steps involved in bringing it to fruition. This is particularly true of long-term decisions. If you approach your task like a sprint, it's easy to burn out and lose focus. If instead, you just try to stay in the game, focusing on each next step, you will have a much better chance of achieving your goal.

One of the most important elements of a great decision process is the momentum that comes from feeling happy with your progress. It's what propels you through moments of doubt and helps you to stay focused. When you sprint in your effort, you may have spikes of success and achieve happiness highs. The problem is that when the high burns out, the momentum quickly dissipates, and sometimes fizzles out entirely. If you are on a diet and sprint, eating nothing but grapefruit for two weeks, you will experience rapid and exciting success. A grapefruit diet isn't sustainable, so at the end of two weeks you may try to switch to a more balanced meal plan, but your results will seem frustratingly slow and demotivating in comparison. It becomes way too tempting to fall off the wagon. Steady, consistent effort gives you even doses of success and is much more conducive to building steady momentum and happiness.

Build Up Will Power

Some people think that willpower is a substance like energy, and once you use it all up, then you run out of it and get fatigued. An alternate view is that willpower is more like a muscle, and the more you use it, the stronger it gets. Resisting some impulses makes you able to slow down and resist other impulses. The reason for this is psychological – when you demonstrate willpower in one area, you can see and believe that your willpower is strong and you can rely on it more and more.

When you are facing important decisions, you may want to work out your willpower muscle in other, non-related areas before you choose anything. Studies show that if you shop when you have to pee you will be better able to resist impulsive decisions simply because you are resisting the impulse to find a bathroom. You could get the same benefit from doing something positive for yourself that takes willpower, such as going for a run. On the flip-side of this, if you recently put on 5 pounds and you just had a bacon burger for lunch, you may feel like your willpower has abandoned you. If so, then this is not the time to make a big decision. Look for ways that you can build up layers of will power in other areas of your life. This will help you slow down your decisions and allow yourself more time to think.

Feed Your Brain

When your brain is tired, you will be more impulsive. When you are making an important decision, you can energize your brain by increasing your glucose levels with something sweet. Artificial sweeteners won't work since whatever you eat has to have real glucose in it to feed your brain. Any real sugar will do the job.

Be Vigilant about Data and Information

A critical part of your effectiveness is the quality of your data and information. You are amazingly persuasive no matter which side you take on an issue. But in order to really maximize the benefits of your strengths, you need to make sure you are right.

What methods and habits do you have to collect information? This is something you need to be very deliberate about. If you are making decisions for an organization, think through what information you need to maximize the quality of those decisions. Where can you get your information, and how often should you get updates? How reliable are your sources?

You need to plan your ongoing data collection with the idea that you need to be battle-ready at any time. Don't wait for the decision meeting and rely on others there to share information with you. Because you are a great talker, you may not be a great listener. You need to master the information on your own. Make data collection a priority in how you perform your work. Do this by allocating a set percentage of your time to data collecting, and by establishing habits and systems that enable you to get the information that you need regularly. You need to be more informed than anyone else because you are more persuasive than anyone else.

Rank the Problem and Set Aside Resources You'll Need

You are an abstract, theoretical thinker. You have a natural ability to see the big picture. So in your effort to balance out your style and develop a middle speed, try adding some strategies that take a more tangible, concrete approach.

Start with the reason for your decision – with the problem you are trying to solve. Define the problem as clearly as you can so that it stays present in your mind over time and demands your focus. Try to visualize those moments when you experience the problem most. Don't start looking at solutions until you can clearly and succinctly define the problem.

Next, evaluate how much pain the problem will cause – not just right now, but over time, and rank it on a scale of one to ten. Is it more or less critical than other things you are working on? Make sure this isn't a self-solving problem that will resolve naturally if you can wait it out. If the pain is sustained over time and it makes sense to move ahead, then start to describe what success would look like.

Get very clear on what is most important for success. Define this success, its specific conditions, as narrowly as you can, and make these few conditions your priority. Try to attach a number to success – would it enable 20% more productivity? Would it double the revenue from one customer? The goal here is to give you something really tangible and concrete to focus on in order to help you create sustained motivation to solve the problem.

Finally, when you are evaluating different solutions, focus on your resources. You may be tempted to overestimate resources that you will have in the future – to double count money or time, and over commit yourself and others. Don't make a commitment until you have the resources in place and set aside, including time or money, to fulfill that commitment. Always assume that whatever you are committing to will take twice as many resources as you expect.

CHAPTER 16

The Experimenting Soul

Pushing action forward

Does This Sound Like You?

Are you drawn to exploration and adventure? Do you drive somewhat aggressively? Do you feel satisfaction and take pride in self-discipline? If you answered yes to at least two of these questions, then you've probably found the right soul type.

What You Are Best At

Your Experimenting decision process is how you get things started quickly and build momentum – you like to get moving and preserve the freedom to improvise as needed. Your skills are invaluable in fast changing environments, in an emergency or under deadlines, where you need logical reasoning and immediate action. While you welcome new ideas and approaches, you have a talent for quickly discerning and understanding the few critical actions or pieces of information that matter most, so you can make judgements quickly and get moving.

What Your Decision Process Looks Like

You like to chart your own course, so your path won't be limited to the boundaries and rules that confine most people. Compared to the Baseline Style of Decision

Making, and the long time it takes to go up and over the hill in Stage 2, you will spend the least amount of time possible in Stage 2. You need less time to make an accurate judgement. You will go around the hill, skipping the rest of Stage 2 and all of Stage 3, and head straight to the edge of the decision. That edge is often where you will stop.

Your style is fast, action oriented, and embraces risk. You prefer to get moving as quickly as possible, which means avoiding a theoretical discussion and putting a solution into action to see how it works. However, this doesn't mean that you will be ready to fully commit to one solution and leap across the canyon. You are more of a bungee jumper. You are happy to leap, but you want to be able to keep your options open, bounce back and choose something else if you need to, just in case the solution you try first doesn't work out. You experiment with solutions, and you trust your ability to adapt, improvise or change course as needed.

YOUR EXPERIMENTING DECISION PROCESS
Your Experimenting decision process jumps right in to test the best available solution,
but leaves your options open so that you can adapt along the way.

In any problem you face, you will plunge right in, get your hands dirty, and then move on to the next thing. This style is not for planners. For you, too much planning feels like a frustrating waste of time. You want to evaluate your options as quickly as possible, which means a heavy dose of skepticism, a lean and fast analysis, a critical eye, and filtering for only the most reliable data. Once you target the solution that looks most promising, you will want to immediately test it out. Unlike other soul types that want to theorize the outcome of multiple options before proceeding, you feel like the best way to know how something will work is to get moving and do it. This is your Experimental decision process at work.

Your decision process makes you perfectly suited to environments that require a rapid response. You are rarely locked into any solution. You are always scanning and comparing to find something better, so when your environment or your needs change, you are the first to see this and the first to adapt and change your approach.

You have an amazing amount of stamina and energy in general, and when combined with your bias toward action, you are a powerhouse of momentum. You have the power to get any project started and keep it moving, which can carry other, more reluctant decision makers forward and create real progress.

Where Doubt Creeps In

Your Experimenting decision process can make quick, accurate judgements and get moving faster than any other soul type – the momentum you bring to the beginning of a solution is invaluable. Your decision process gives you a fantastic ability to adapt and drive change as soon as it's needed. However, the sacrifice you make for all that speed is that you might never fully commit to any choice, so you might find that you are dissatisfied with whatever choice you make.

You stay in a constant state of testing. You are constantly evaluating the choice you made with a critical eye, looking for what isn't good about it, and scanning for something that might be better.

The problem this creates is that staying in comparison-mode after you have made your choice can make you like your choice less and less. With each comparison, the benefits you liked before will seem less impactful, and you will focus more and more on its faults. Instead of building energy around the best option, you might dissipate your momentum by pulling focus away from the choice you are testing and bringing other options into play, never building up enough momentum behind any one option to really commit to it. This can mean a lot of wasted energy as you pull your focus (and the focus of anyone who is following you) from idea to idea in a constant state of urgent testing and evaluation. When this happens, you open yourself up to doubt, which means that not only are you less satisfied with your choices, but you are less effective than you could be.

Notes on Reducing Your Doubt

To get the most out of your decision style, you need to keep your ability to get things started, and learn some new strategies to keep your momentum and focus it behind one best choice so that you can commit and start to feel more satisfied with your choices.

Taking the Tags Off

When you buy something, if you really want to be happy with your purchase, you have to take the tags off and commit to it. Unfortunately, not every choice you make comes with the convenient commitment-mechanism of purchase tags. Taking the tags off is a metaphor for cancelling your option to reverse your commitment. When a decision matters and is impactful to your happiness, you need to take whatever step you need to get fully invested in your choice. The first steps are to give up your alternate choices and burn any bridges, which means to give up any ways of reversing or cancelling your commitment. In addition, you can also work to become more emotionally invested in your choice.

Invest in Your Choice

Being a disciplined person is something you find rewarding, so it might help for you to apply your natural desire to find fulfillment in working hard at something. Can you find a way to invest in your decision in a way that requires discipline and hard work? For example, you might feel better about your car purchase if you decide to keep it immaculately clean all the time. You might find a relationship more fulfilling if you take up distance running together.

You can also invest yourself in your choice in a way that makes it painful if you change your mind. If you told me that you wanted to lose five pounds, I would ask you to think of a political cause that you truly dislike. I would then ask you to write a check to that organization for $500.00 and give it to me. I would call you in six weeks, and if you had lost the five pounds, I would tear up the check and you would get to keep your money. If you didn't lose the weight, I would send the check to the offending cause and your money would be gone. The only way to keep your money is to complete your goal.

Your chances of losing weight if we do this are five times greater than if you set out to lose weight on your own. When you write the check, you are making it painful for yourself to change your mind. It isn't something you're just experimenting with. You have truly decided to lose weight, and you have made an irreversible commitment. If you want to do this in real life, there are ways to help yourself. For example, you can sign up for a goal setting service such as the one at www.stickK.com. I would wish you luck, but if you are making a true commitment you probably won't need it.

Stay Focused

For many people, when they are worried about a problem, it feels better to be doing something instead of nothing because doing something increases the feeling of control. If the stakes are high and the decision is risky, it's very hard to stand still. The more worried we are, the more we want control, and the more we will be tempted to take action. This is called the *action bias*, also known as *Ants in Your Pants*.[vi]

Professional soccer players get ants in their pants. They know that the best strategy to block a penalty kick is for the goalkeeper to stay in the middle of the goal, which gives him the best chance of blocking the ball. Despite this, in an analysis of 286 penalty kicks in top soccer leagues and championships, it was found that the professional goalies almost always jumped right or left. When the stakes are high, waiting for the ball just doesn't feel right.

It's ironic that the desire to be doing something can keep us from getting things done. I've frequently seen this with leaders in large organizations. If the leader's job is to determine the strategy for the organization, ideally that leader will determine what to do, communicate the strategy, and patiently coax it along as the contributors in the organization execute and do their work. Most of the time, the leader will feel great at the beginning of this process when she is developing and communicating her strategy. She will feel like things are moving, and that she is in control. However, once it is time for the strategy to begin its slow percolation through the organization, she has to be patient and let the work happen.

This makes many leaders panic. They can't stand to wait in the middle of the goal box for the ball to come. They have to jump right or left. Sometimes they decide that the strategy they came up with wasn't good enough and they start the process over again with a new, better strategy. Sometimes it means that they drop the effort and run to the next problem that grabs their attention, taking everyone with them. Either way, lots of planning happens, but no actual work can get done. This leaves the organization stuck in Stages 1 and 2, forever deciding what to do but not committing to any one effort.

Complex decisions can take a long time. When the process and the action steps unfold slowly, remain focused on them. Apply consistent pressure to see the process and steps through. Part of success is keeping the momentum going for others by keeping your attention on the problem until completion.

CHAPTER 17

The Collaborative Soul

Pulling people together

Does This Sound Like You?

Do you offer your time to help, teach, or organize others? Do you feel energized when you're around groups of people? Are you sentimental about things, objects, or people from your past? If you answered yes to at least two of these questions, then you've probably found the right soul type.

What You Are Best At

The Collaborative soul type pulls people together, creating communities and connections. You step into this leading role through the integrity of your actions. You strive to set a perfect example, modeling the same behaviors that you want to see in others and that bind a team, group or community together. You support and reinforce the morals, structure, mission, and growth of the communities that you belong to. It's as if you are the moral center or heart of any group, a lighthouse that all the other members can navigate towards to connect with the community and find their way home.

Your natural perspective in all things is to think about the greater good. You gravitate to ideas and missions that raise all boats in a rising tide, and you prioritize the needs of the community above the interests any individual. You value and respect the morals, rules and traditions of the communities, groups or culture that you belong to and expect others to do the same.

You have the highest standards for yourself and others, and you are constantly striving to be and do better. You want to push beyond any self-limitations. You support the mission of the teams and communities that you are part of with determined hard work, and others count on you to pitch in wherever you're needed. You are the one who shows up early to set up for the meeting and stays late to clean up.

You temper your high expectations with emotional vulnerability that makes you immensely likeable, although probably not great at poker. You wear your heart on your sleeve. You openly show your enthusiasm and zeal, seeing miracles all around you and inspiring others with your positive thinking.

What Your Decision Process Looks Like

Your style is ready for fun and adventure as long as you can be cautious and responsible. You will gravitate toward solutions that are less likely to create ambiguity, disagreement, or conflict. So you may prefer traditional approaches to doing new things and familiar or proven ways of solving problems. You may feel more comfortable with rules and structure since they help to clarify expectations and reduce uncertainty.

Your decisions will have strong momentum from your own enthusiasm, but will proceed at an even, cautious pace through the four decision making stages. You don't want to be rushed. You need time to consider your options and think them through.

You most likely find the opinions presented by experts and authorities to be very helpful, as are case studies, examples where your solution was used effectively, and any personal experience you may have. You prefer to let others forge new trails, and you will follow once you see that everything worked out well for them.

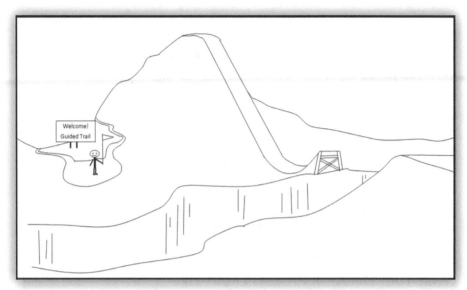

YOUR COLLABORATIVE DECISION PROCESS

Your Collaborative Soul type is inspirational, emphasizes teamwork,
working with and learning from others, and tends to prefer traditional approaches.

The balance you strike in your decision making lies between enthusiasm and caution. This makes you exceptionally good at pulling people together. Your buoyant, genuine passion draws people in, and your cautious approach enables you to build consensus around ideas and minimize conflict.

Where Doubt Creeps In

Your Collaborative decision process is even and cautious, so there aren't any obvious gaps in how you work through choices. Your decision making skills are excellent, and the only thing getting in your way is your fear of making a mistake. You may be very focused on avoiding buyer's remorse, and that worry may actually cause some amount of doubt and remorse for you after your decision. Too much of your focus is on what could go wrong, instead of the things that are right about your choice.

Notes on Reducing Your Doubt

You will benefit by getting more comfortable with failure and negative feedback. Make room for *constructive conflict,* and learn not to stay longer than you should.

Get More Comfortable with Failure and Negative Feedback

Failure happens to everyone, and it's a sign that you are stretching yourself and doing things that make you grow. Yet, avoiding failure drives you. You hold yourself to a very high standard and you work very hard to minimize risk of failure. You exceed everyone's expectations most of the time. So when you don't succeed or when you receive negative feedback about something, this can hit you hard. As much as failure or feedback can hurt, they are both valuable gifts. Failures and feedback teach us faster and more effectively than anything else. If you don't know where you are going wrong, it's very hard to grow and get better, and even the best of us have room to improve.

Try changing the way you thing about feedback and failure. Make it a goal to fail quickly. The sooner you get feedback, the faster you adapt and learn, and the better your chances are at success. Approaching your decisions with the attitude that failure is just a helpful nudge in the right direction takes the sting out of it and gets you where you want to go faster.

Make Room for Constructive Conflict

When there is conflict surrounding a decision it may make you really uncomfortable. When no one agrees on the best way to succeed, it's hard to know how to best avoid failure. You may feel like conflict adds ambiguity to the problem and the heated emotions that can come out of these discussions may give you some anxiety. To avoid this, you might push to get the decision resolved and settle for the most agreeable option or, in the event that getting everyone to agree is too difficult, you may become stuck and let the decision drag on for too long.

The challenge for you is to allow for brainstorming, dialogue, and conflict. Inviting stakeholders to challenge ideas, to discuss issues and negative implications, will give you greater alignment and harmony in the final result. Even though conflict feels uncomfortable, it's a necessary part of finding agreement – you have to work your way through the conflict in order to get there. When people are required to compromise, they need the opportunity to be heard first and to feel that their opinion and perspective has been considered. By making room for everyone to air their disagreements, you are enabling them to set aside their differences.

Staying Longer Than You Should

You may be a nostalgic person. Your past may have an even rosier glow now than it did when you were living it. This is a positive in terms of your general happiness, but it's also something to be aware of when you're deciding to make changes. If you are attached to decisions that you made in the past, you might not adapt or change those decisions quickly enough. Decisions have different life spans, and if a decision becomes very personal, it's possible that you could end up pushing it long past its expiration date. Think of someone who is still wearing his hair the way he did in high school because it became part of his self-identity, despite the mounting evidence that mullets are no longer fashionable.

On a larger scale, this same thing happens in the corporate world. When a company experiences success and becomes a market leader, such as IBM did in its golden decade of the 1960's, the positive experience of winning can magnify that company's commitment to its existing business model. Employees identify with the experience of winning, and there is tremendous social support for decisions that reinforce the status quo. When bad news arrives that contradicts their current business model, the company only hears what it wants to hear. IBM remained blind to the importance of software, even as Bill Gates and his buddies ran off with the rights to make billions.

Why didn't Kodak capitalize on digital photography? Kodak was just too invested in film and printing, so its digital camera technology got put aside. Why didn't Sony's Walkman become the iPod? Why didn't Blockbuster become Netflix? At some point companies like these realize that they need to change, but usually they are so late to the party that they miss the boat.

Being on top is a mixed blessing. It comes with the risk that we become so proud of what we've done that we fail to see when tastes, trends, and the environment are changing around us. If you are still wearing a mullet, it's probably because, at one time, your mullet was really, really cool. Business in the front, and weekend in the back – what's not to like? It's great to love your choices, but you also have to keep a close eye on what's coming and be ready to adapt.

Look for the Life Span of Your Decision

How long should the life span of a decision be? If you are buying a new sofa, how long do you expect it last, and when should you revisit the sofa decision? Sofa manufacturers claim a life span 7 years, so it's reasonable to think that you'll inspect your sofa for mystery stains and saggy cushions after 7 years and potentially move it to the basement. Charitably, your wardrobe should probably be questioned at least every decade. In business, determining the life span of your business model is crucial for your responsiveness to changing market conditions and for your ongoing success. Which aspects of your business model are vulnerable? What emerging trends could impact you?

Part Five
Final Thoughts

CHAPTER 18

Dealing With Fear And Anxiety

There may be some areas of your life where you generally feel more worry or anxiety. For example, some people have fears about running out of money, or about getting sick, or they are afraid of losing love and being abandoned. These kinds of deeper fears or worries are different from the general ambiguity that we talked about in Chapter 2 because they aren't specific to any one situation or decision. They are part of how you have been experiencing your life.

If you experience a fear or anxiety like this, it can affect any decisions that you make in that area of your life. For those decisions, you might find that your normal process changes and becomes more conservative and cautious. Like all decision processes, this altered version of your process has its own strengths and weaknesses.

The Good and The Bad

Generally we think of fear as something negative to be conquered, however fear isn't always bad. In the right circumstances and in small doses it looks like caution or prudence, and it can play a constructive role in your decision making. In the wild, fear helps to protect you from being eaten by bears. In your living room, fear prevents you from buying everything on QVC. Constructive fear can help to balance out any impulsive pushes for novelty and change and provides a stabilizing influence that helps to makes sure you aren't throwing the baby out with the bathwater.

When a small, measured dose of fear is added to your decision making, you might adapt your decision process in order to mitigate your risks and keep the benefits of continuity. Too much change can lead to a lack of distinct process, as well as heightened anxiety, and a lot of wasted effort. A little bit of well-placed fear can emphasize the value of what you currently have, which help to keep people and their communities together, maintain traditions, and increase the feeling of safety. It focuses you on keeping the solutions that are working already, and their existing momentum.

However, the biggest drawback to making decisions under the influence of too much fear is that it takes you out of flow. The ambiguity caused by change can cause you to feel a loss of control, and you may respond by exerting control where you can rather than allowing your life to unfold naturally. You may want to change only what is necessary, look for familiar solutions and work to lock things down and get closure. You may want to settle as soon as a logical option is found. These are protective strategies, and while they mitigate risk, they can also limit you.

How Fear Might Impact Your Decision Process

Constructive fear helps you to look ahead at the beginning of a decision to think through and prepare for the possible risks and dangers that could come your way. The focus is on *minimizing risks*, so once you enter into a decision process you may look for the nearest acceptable solution.

This means that your decision process may alter to resemble a shortened version the Baseline Decision Making Process, with fewer options to consider and less deliberation time. Under the influence of fear, Stage 1 can be long, but you might compress or bypass the remaining decision stages altogether, instead choosing the fastest available route back to a place of stability and closure.

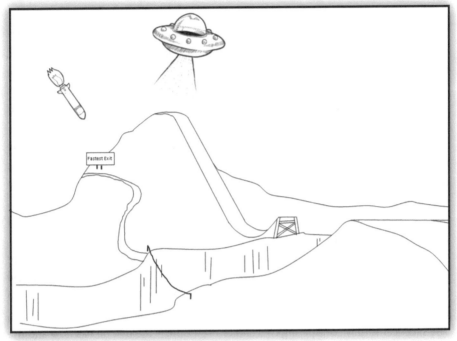

HOW FEAR IMPACTS YOUR DECISIONS

*Fear motivates you to minimize risks and
resolve any open decision process as quickly as possible.*

Because you narrow your focus when you feel fear and are oriented toward managing risk, you can become better at quickly breaking down complicated ideas and classifying your options. You may seek lots of data and detail when you are in Stage 1, and this can be a lot to work with. But fear motivates you to process all this data in a narrow, focused way that gets right down to what is essential for your analysis.

At the end of your careful thought process, since you are trying to manage your own perception of risk, you will probably make decisions with your gut.

When Fear Takes Over

To help prevent fear from taking over too much of your decision process, you may want to deliberately take time to explore your alternatives and let go of any idealized, unattainable options.

Explore Your Options

When you are feeling fear, you tend to limit the number of alternatives you consider and to set realistic goals for yourself. These are strategies that can lead to feeling good about your decisions, but if taken too far, they can limit your potential and deprive you of a fuller life experience. When limiting alternatives and goals is taken too far, it's called *satisficing*.[vii] The defining feature of satisficing is how you find and weigh your alternatives.

If someone is trying to find the optimal decision, looking for the best possible solution, they will reach out to find many alternatives, and then narrow their decision down to the four or five that they will evaluate and consider. They will compare the four or five alternatives to each other at the same time, looking for the pros and cons of each. This increases the likelihood that many factors will be considered, weighed and ranked, resulting in a better decision.

By contrast, when someone is satisficing in decision making, he will take a more passive approach to finding alternatives. He will wait until he stumbles upon a new alternative, like a hermit crab finding a new shell. He will then compare this alternative to his current solution, and will decide if it is better or worse than what he already has. The satisficer is only considering two choices at a time – the one he has now and the new one he found. This means that the new option doesn't have to be the best option – it just has to be better than what he has now. The new option has to pass a minimum threshold. If this satisficing decision habit is applied repeatedly in someone's life, in areas that are impactful, that person will have a life that only meets the minimum threshold of what he could possibly hope for.

Imagine a recent college graduate who has been bagging groceries to earn extra money while he was in school. Now that he has graduated, he is facing an intimidating job hunt. The manager of the grocery store decides to offer him a position as a cashier at the store, which pays much more than most entry level jobs, but has more limited upside potential. If you were searching for the optimal job, you would evaluate the opportunity by comparing it against several other options, and would most likely weigh any (if any) long-term career potential more highly than the possibility of an immediate income boost. A satisficer, on the other hand, will only compare the cashier position to his current state, which is a part-time grocery bagger looking for a job. The cashier position will win, and the college grad will miss out on whatever other opportunities may have been on his horizon.

When you rush towards closure, not only are you missing out on potential opportunity, but it also introduces doubt and ambiguity into your decisions after they are made because you cut your process too short. In order for you to feel confident about your choices, you have to take the time to explore your options. Make a point of evaluating at least three logical options, and thinking through their long-term implications, before you decide to choose one.

Let Go of Idealized, Unattainable Options

If you have a dream or ideal you don't pursue, either commit to it or give it up. It is standing between you and your happiness.

I had a friend who kept a photo on his refrigerator of the one that got away– the girl he'd met in Germany years ago. She had moved on, had a child, and lived her life. But he was still exchanging letters with her and keeping her photo there to remind him that perfection was possible. Whenever he started to develop a relationship with someone else, he would compare this new girlfriend to the German girl. He would think of all the many amazing attributes of the seemingly flawless German girl. These attributes would flower into an undefeatable, 450-pound gorilla of feminine wiles that would crush her poor opponent who by this point couldn't even eat her salad right.

German-girl was his one-in-the-wings. She was his idealized dream that kept him from having to fully invest in the real life that he had. He had spent years comparing his dates to an idealized, almost imaginary woman. As a result he was perpetually dissatisfied with every date he had. As far as I know, he is still single.

The one in the wings can be any option or idea that we keep and hold on to, but never pursue. It can be anything from a long-desired trip around the world to a steamy friendship that's loaded with unresolved sexual tension. The purpose of the one in the wings is to protect us from getting hurt or disappointed by the choices we do pursue. It serves as an ideal against which we can compare the options we have chosen. We use it to find fault with our choices so that we feel less vulnerable and exposed to our fear of disappointment, loss, failure or abandonment. It draws us away from commitment just enough so that we never fully get into bed with our choices. It isn't exactly a fallback position, because we never have any real intention of pursuing it.

The one in the wings is special. The reason it is special is because we make it that way. In order for the one in the wings to be sufficiently magnetic to pull us away from our commitment, it has to have something about it that is unique, superior, fabulous and desirable. It also has to be unattainable in some way. We have to keep enough distance from the one in the wings for it to keep its glossy, blemish-free complexion. If we ever make the mistake of getting too close to it, it loses its special powers and becomes just another alternative - maybe not even as good as the one we've already got.

Holding onto unattainable, idealized options is a way of dealing with our fear of decision making. As a delay tactic, it can work wonders for you, but it also can make you miserable. If you have a dream or ideal you don't pursue, either commit to it or give it up. It is standing between you and being in flow.

CHAPTER 19

How To Get Back On Track

Now you have a clear understanding of how doubt creeps into your decision process and how to prevent it. But what if you're already living with a decision, half committed, and full of doubt? What if you're dissatisfied with your job, your relationship, or some other aspect of your life and you wish you weren't?

In order to get back on track, you need to hit a reset button on your Difference Engine. You can do this in two different ways. You can exit the decision you're in and start over again from the beginning, or you can get emotionally invested in the decision you've made.

Getting emotionally invested is easier than it seems at first. It's hard to imagine feeling differently than you do right at this moment about whatever is causing you to feel dissatisfied. This is because you experience emotions such as dissatisfaction in a sort of eternal "now". Think about when you're home on your sofa, feeling too tired and antisocial to go to a party you've been invited to. When you're sitting in your sweats on your sofa, it's really hard to imagine the feeling of having fun at the party. You can only feel what you feel right in that moment, which is tired and anti-social. Your logical mind can make you get up and go, but it's a struggle. Then, once you get to the party, you feel really happy you went. You're suddenly energized and having fun, and you can't imagine sitting at home on your sofa. Emotions are like that. They can only experience what is true right in that moment. So, when you're dissatisfied and feeling doubt about something in your life, it's hard to imagine ever feeling really great about it. However, changing how you feel is possible with a little effort.

If you want to feel differently about some circumstance, thing or person in your life, you can make that happen by investing some part of yourself in a way that makes you feel good about you.

I watched an old French movie once about an older couple that wasn't very happy. The husband felt like he didn't love his wife anymore. Then she became ill, and he took care of her, and through the process of caring for her, he fell in love with her again. It wasn't a great movie, and please don't get sick just to spice up your romance, but it was an example of what I'm talking about. We care about the things that we take care of. When you take care of things, you invest yourself, and that helps you to make the emotional commitment you need to make in order to free yourself from doubt.

To make this really work for you, it's best if you can get actively engaged in some creative problem solving, using those skills that your soul type is best at. A Coaching soul who wants to feel differently about their job might see if there is someone at work who they can mentor. An Optimizing soul who wants to feel differently about their house might rearrange the furniture, or add something to it that is unique and personal.

My husband and I recently bought a small vacation house that is almost falling down. It's a project, but we were drawn to it because it has the potential to be fantastic if we put in some work. Actually, a lot of work. The problem is that we are pretty busy with a family and two careers, and after buying it we started to spiral into cycles of doubt. We thought about selling, then decided to keep it, then thought about selling again. We were wasting time and emotional energy, and needed to get recommitted to our choice.

We started investing ourselves into the project. We began some demolition work, getting the place cleaned up, and I drew up a floor plan that we both liked. We started imagining what the place would be like when it was all done and we could spend weekends there with our family. To make it feel more real, we bought a small hibachi and invited some friends to the property for a rustic hotdog barbeque. Now we're excited about the project and moving full steam ahead, which is a lot less work than spinning in circles, worrying about what to do.

Invest some part of yourself in the things you want to feel good about. Then, to keep that good feeling, be careful not to re-open the decision in your mind. Remember that the three critical steps to making a commitment are to make a decision, give up the alternatives, and burn your bridges. It's an exclusionary process. This means don't stop and walk through the open houses that are for sale if you're trying to stay satisfied with where you live. Don't peruse job listings online if you want to stay engaged at work. Re-opening your decision by introducing new alternatives is opening yourself up to doubt and dissatisfaction. This is fine if you're really ready for a change, but if you truly want to or need to stay with the status quo, renew your commitment and stop shopping.

CHAPTER 20

Undoubtedly Awesome

When two people with the same soul type meet, they might click right away and find that it's easy to talk or work together because they see the world from a similar vantage point. They approach problem solving in the same way, with shared priorities.

At the same time, they may find that they are very different from each other, and that the choices they make for their individual lives don't seem to have a lot in common. This is not surprising, as a particular soul type and decision process is one small aspect of that person's behavior.

Your personality, your culture, and your environment can all play a part in the choices you make. In the end, your own specific decision process is unique to you. So when you select from the preceding chapters the soul type that fits you best and read about its various characteristics, you know this is just part of the picture. The rest of who you are as a person then forms the rest of the picture.

These other parts of you also come into play when you are struggling with doubt. You may have personal or cultural beliefs or environmental habits that cause you to feel more doubt in some situations. The descriptions and suggestions I've written about in this book won't address every moment of doubt you have. However, this book does give you a framework for understanding and interpreting your own experience of doubt. It can help you to see yourself more clearly so that you recognize when your decision process is creating more doubt for you.

Once you understand your soul type as I've described it, you might start to notice the ways in which you are different. You might notice places where you experience doubt that don't seem to come from your decisions, or that come from decision behaviors I haven't described. You might see beliefs you have that create doubt for you.

Hopefully this book will provide enough of a framework so that other aspects of yourself such as these can become clearer as well.

This awareness and self-understanding is the way to reduce your doubt and get into flow. Our thoughts create our reality, and when your thoughts reflect confidence and satisfaction in the choices you've made and the life you are creating for yourself, what comes next in your life will be undoubtedly awesome.

i   Querstret, D., & Cropley, M. (2013). Assessing treatments used to reduce rumination and/or worry: A systematic review. Clinical Psychology Review, 33(8), 996-1009. doi:10.1016/j.cpr.2013.08.004

Mclaughlin, K. A., & Nolen-Hoeksema, S. (2011). Rumination as a transdiagnostic factor in depression and anxiety. Behaviour Research and Therapy, 49(3), 186-193. doi:10.1016/j.brat.2010.12.006

ii   Wilcox, B. W. (2013). If You Want a Prenup, You Don't Want Marriage. New York Times. April 5, 2013. <http://www.nytimes.com/roomfordebate/2013/03/21/thepower- of-the-prenup/if-you-want-a-prenup-you-dont-want-marriage>

The National Marriage Project. Knot Yet: The Benefits and Costs of Delayed Marriage in America. < http://twentysomethingmarriage.org>

iii   Ericson, K. M., & Fuster, A. (2013). The endowment effect. Cambridge, MA.

Thaler, R. H. (n.d.). Misbehaving: The making of behavioral economics.

Thaler, R. H., & Sunstein, C. R. (2008). Nudge: Improving decisions about health, wealth, and happiness. New Haven, CT: Yale University Press.

iv   Fisher, B.A. and Ellis, D. "Anatomy of Communication in Decision-Making Groups: Improving Effectiveness," in Fisher, B. A. (1990). Small Group Decision Making. 3d ed., McGraw-Hill, New York. 170-200.

v   Iyengar, S. S. and Lepper, M.R. (2000). When choice is demotivating: Can one desire too much of a good thing? Journal of Personality and Social Psychology 79(6), 995.1006.

Iyengar, S. S. and Kamenica, E. (2010). Choice proliferation, simplicity seeking, and asset allocation. Journal of Public Economics 94(7-8), 530.539.

vi   Bar-Eli, M., and Azar, O.H., and Ritov, I, Keidar-Levin, Y. and Schein. G. (2007). Action bias among elite soccer goalkeepers: The case of penalty kicks. Journal of Economic Psychology. Volume 28, Issue 5, October. 606-621.

vii   Etzioni, A. (1988). *The Moral Dimension: Toward a New Economics.* New York: The Free Press.

About the Author

Anne Tucker

Anne is an effective and recognized speaker who has addressed audiences around the world on the topics of leadership, personal transformation, decision making, and the psychology of doubt. She is the founder of Wisdom Soup, an online social learning community that speeds up serendipity by connecting people with similar interests in spirituality and personal growth.

Decision making has been the ongoing focus of Anne's 20 year career, during which she has worked with some of the most influential business leaders of our time. Anne developed her methodology for understanding decision making by soul type during her years as the co-founder of Grey Matter Partners, a leadership development firm based in Seattle, Washington, where she worked with senior executives and others, teaching a coaching process that one client referred to as his "awakening." Anne's clients are able to reduce ambiguity for themselves and their organizations, see their strengths and opportunities with more clarity, and move forward on an ever more clear path to achieving their goals.

www.AnneTucker.com